**TEACHER'S PET PUBLICATIONS**

PUZZLE PACK
for
Frankenstein

based on the book by
Mary Shelley

Written by
William T. Collins

© 2005 Teacher's Pet Publications
All Rights Reserved

The materials in this packet are copyrighted
by Teacher's Pet Publications, Inc.

These pages may be duplicated by the purchaser
for use in the purchaser's own classroom.

Copying any of these materials and distributing them
for any other purpose is a violation of the copyright laws.

© 2005 Teacher's Pet Publications, Inc.
www.tpet.com

INTRODUCTION
If you already own the LitPlan for this title, this Puzzle Pack will refresh your Unit Resource Materials and Vocabulary Resource Materials sections plus give you additional materials you can substitute into the tests. If you do not already have a complete LitPlan, these pages will give you some supplemental materials to use with your own plan. There are two main groups of materials: one set for unit words (such as characters' names, symbols, places, etc.) and one set for vocabulary words associated with the book.

WORD LIST
There is a word list for both the unit words and the vocabulary words. These lists show you which words are being used in the materials and the clues or definitions being used for those words. You may want to give students a word list with clues/definitions to help them, or you may want students to only have a word list (without clues/definitions) if you want them to work a little harder. Both are available for duplication. The word lists can also be your "calling key" for the bingo games.

FILL IN THE BLANK AND MATCHING
There are 4 each of the fill in the blank and matching worksheets for both the unit and vocabulary words. These pages can be used either as extra worksheets for students or as objective parts of a unit test. They can be done individually if students need extra help or as a whole class activity to review the material covered.

MAGIC SQUARES
The magic squares not only reinforce the material covered but also work on reasoning and math skills. Many teachers have told us that their students really enjoy doing these!

WORD SEARCH PUZZLES
The word search words go in all directions, as indicated on your answer keys. Two of the word search puzzles have the clues listed rather than the words. This makes the puzzle a little more difficult, but it reinforces the material better. Two word search puzzles have words only for students who find the clue puzzles too difficult.

CROSSWORD PUZZLES
Both unit and vocabulary word sections have 4 crossword puzzles.

BINGO CARDS
There are 32 individual bingo cards for the unit words and 32 individual bingo cards for the vocabulary words. You can use your word list as a "call list," calling the words at random and marking them off of your list as you go, or you could use the flash cards by cutting them apart and drawing the words at random from a hat (or box or whatever). To make a better review, you might ask for the definition and spelling of each word as you call it out—or you could call out the definitions and have students tell you the words they need to look for on the puzzle.

JUGGLE LETTERS
The vocabulary juggle letter game is intended to help students learn the spellings of the words. One sheet has the definitions listed on it as an extra help for students who need it or to reinforce the definitions if you choose to do so.

FLASH CARDS
We've included a set of vocabulary flash cards you can duplicate, cut, and fold for your students. Some teachers make a few sets for general use by the class; others make a set for each student. Some teachers duplicate them for each student and have the students cut & fold their own. You can cut out just the words and put them in a hat, have each student pick out one word and write the definition and a sentence for that word. Students then swap words and papers, with the next student adding a sentence of his own under the last one. You can have students swap as many times as you like. Each time the student will read the sentences written prior to his own and then add a sentence. You can cut out the words and definitions separately and play "I Have; Who Has?" Each student in the room draws a word and definition. The first student says, "I have (the name of the word). Who has the definition?" The student with the definition reads it then says, "I have (the name of the vocabulary word she has). Who has the definition?" The round continues until all words and definitions have been given.

Frankenstein Word List

No.	Word	Clue/Definition
1.	ALPHONSE	Died of grief
2.	ALPS	Meeting site for creature and creator
3.	ARCTIC	Creature last seen here
4.	BYRON	Proposed writing ghost stories; Lord ___
5.	CAROLINE	Frankenstein matriarch; ___ Beaufort
6.	CHEMISTRY	Subject studied by Victor
7.	CONFUSION	Creature's first feeling
8.	CORNELIUS	Influential author; ___ Agrippa
9.	CREATURE	Miserable wretch
10.	DISGUST	Frankenstein's feeling after the creation
11.	ELIZABETH	Married Victor; ___ Lavenza
12.	ENGLAND	Destination of letters
13.	ERNEST	Wanted military career; ___ Frankenstein
14.	FELIX	Taught Safie and the creature; ___ De Lacey
15.	FEMALE	Creature's request of Frankenstein
16.	FOOD	Hard for creature to find
17.	FRANKENSTEIN	Title of the book
18.	FRIENDSHIP	Creature wanted this from humans
19.	GENEVA	Home of Frankenstein family
20.	GUILTY	Verdict at Justine's trial
21.	HENRY	Frankenstein's best friend; ___ Clerval
22.	INGOLSTADT	Site of original creation
23.	INNOCENT	Verdict at Victor's trial
24.	KIRWIN	Friendly Irish magistrate
25.	KREMPE	Unfriendly professor
26.	LACEY	Creature asked for his friendship; M. De ___
27.	LETTERS	Intended for Margaret Saville
28.	LIFE	What Frankenstein wanted to create
29.	LIGHT	Uncomfortable for creature at first
30.	LOCKET	Incriminating evidence
31.	MARY	Author of Frankenstein; ___ Shelley
32.	MORITZ	Wrongly executed; Justine ___
33.	OBSERVATION	How creature learned about humans
34.	PERCY	His discussions influenced his wife
35.	PROMETHEUS	Frankenstein compared to him
36.	READ	What Felix taught creature to do
37.	REMORSE	Frankenstein's feeling about Justine
38.	SAFIE	Left father to marry Felix
39.	SCARLET	Killed Victor's mother; ___ fever
40.	SCOTLAND	Frankenstein abandoned creation plans here
41.	THREE	Number of the creature's victims
42.	VICTOR	The creator
43.	WALDMAN	Introduced Victor to natural philosophy
44.	WALTON	Rescued Frankenstein; Robert ___
45.	WILLIAM	First victim; ___ Frankenstein

Frankenstein Fill In The Blank 1

_____ 1. Number of the creature's victims

_____ 2. Introduced Victor to natural philosophy

_____ 3. Verdict at Victor's trial

_____ 4. Friendly Irish magistrate

_____ 5. Left father to marry Felix

_____ 6. Influential author; ____ Agrippa

_____ 7. Author of Frankenstein; ___ Shelley

_____ 8. First victim; _____ Frankenstein

_____ 9. Unfriendly professor

_____ 10. What Frankenstein wanted to create

_____ 11. Verdict at Justine's trial

_____ 12. Creature's request of Frankenstein

_____ 13. Creature last seen here

_____ 14. Title of the book

_____ 15. Wanted military career; _____ Frankenstein

_____ 16. Frankenstein's best friend; ___ Clerval

_____ 17. Frankenstein abandoned creation plans here

_____ 18. Frankenstein's feeling after the creation

_____ 19. How creature learned about humans

_____ 20. Frankenstein's feeling about Justine

Frankenstein Fill In The Blank 1 Answer Key

THREE	1. Number of the creature's victims
WALDMAN	2. Introduced Victor to natural philosophy
INNOCENT	3. Verdict at Victor's trial
KIRWIN	4. Friendly Irish magistrate
SAFIE	5. Left father to marry Felix
CORNELIUS	6. Influential author; ____ Agrippa
MARY	7. Author of Frankenstein; ___ Shelley
WILLIAM	8. First victim; _____ Frankenstein
KREMPE	9. Unfriendly professor
LIFE	10. What Frankenstein wanted to create
GUILTY	11. Verdict at Justine's trial
FEMALE	12. Creature's request of Frankenstein
ARCTIC	13. Creature last seen here
FRANKENSTEIN	14. Title of the book
ERNEST	15. Wanted military career; _____ Frankenstein
HENRY	16. Frankenstein's best friend; ___ Clerval
SCOTLAND	17. Frankenstein abandoned creation plans here
DISGUST	18. Frankenstein's feeling after the creation
OBSERVATION	19. How creature learned about humans
REMORSE	20. Frankenstein's feeling about Justine

Frankenstein Fill In The Blank 2

_____ 1. Proposed writing ghost stories; Lord ___
_____ 2. Verdict at Victor's trial
_____ 3. Hard for creature to find
_____ 4. Frankenstein matriarch; ____ Beaufort
_____ 5. Wrongly executed; Justine ___
_____ 6. Friendly Irish magistrate
_____ 7. Site of original creation
_____ 8. Uncomfortable for creature at first
_____ 9. Verdict at Justine's trial
_____ 10. The creator
_____ 11. Destination of letters
_____ 12. Incriminating evidence
_____ 13. Died of grief
_____ 14. Killed Victor's mother; ____ fever
_____ 15. Meeting site for creature and creator
_____ 16. Married Victor; ___ Lavenza
_____ 17. Author of Frankenstein; ___ Shelley
_____ 18. Left father to marry Felix
_____ 19. Creature last seen here
_____ 20. His discussions influenced his wife

Frankenstein Fill In The Blank 2 Answer Key

BYRON	1. Proposed writing ghost stories; Lord ___
INNOCENT	2. Verdict at Victor's trial
FOOD	3. Hard for creature to find
CAROLINE	4. Frankenstein matriarch; ___ Beaufort
MORITZ	5. Wrongly executed; Justine ___
KIRWIN	6. Friendly Irish magistrate
INGOLSTADT	7. Site of original creation
LIGHT	8. Uncomfortable for creature at first
GUILTY	9. Verdict at Justine's trial
VICTOR	10. The creator
ENGLAND	11. Destination of letters
LOCKET	12. Incriminating evidence
ALPHONSE	13. Died of grief
SCARLET	14. Killed Victor's mother; ___ fever
ALPS	15. Meeting site for creature and creator
ELIZABETH	16. Married Victor; ___ Lavenza
MARY	17. Author of Frankenstein; ___ Shelley
SAFIE	18. Left father to marry Felix
ARCTIC	19. Creature last seen here
PERCY	20. His discussions influenced his wife

Frankenstein Fill In The Blank 3

1. What Frankenstein wanted to create
2. Verdict at Justine's trial
3. Introduced Victor to natural philosophy
4. Incriminating evidence
5. Friendly Irish magistrate
6. Hard for creature to find
7. Killed Victor's mother; ____ fever
8. Died of grief
9. Number of the creature's victims
10. How creature learned about humans
11. Married Victor; ____ Lavenza
12. Meeting site for creature and creator
13. Rescued Frankenstein; Robert ____
14. Site of original creation
15. What Felix taught creature to do
16. Creature wanted this from humans
17. Proposed writing ghost stories; Lord ____
18. Home of Frankenstein family
19. Creature last seen here
20. Unfriendly professor

Frankenstein Fill In The Blank 3 Answer Key

LIFE	1. What Frankenstein wanted to create
GUILTY	2. Verdict at Justine's trial
WALDMAN	3. Introduced Victor to natural philosophy
LOCKET	4. Incriminating evidence
KIRWIN	5. Friendly Irish magistrate
FOOD	6. Hard for creature to find
SCARLET	7. Killed Victor's mother; ____ fever
ALPHONSE	8. Died of grief
THREE	9. Number of the creature's victims
OBSERVATION	10. How creature learned about humans
ELIZABETH	11. Married Victor; ____ Lavenza
ALPS	12. Meeting site for creature and creator
WALTON	13. Rescued Frankenstein; Robert ____
INGOLSTADT	14. Site of original creation
READ	15. What Felix taught creature to do
FRIENDSHIP	16. Creature wanted this from humans
BYRON	17. Proposed writing ghost stories; Lord ____
GENEVA	18. Home of Frankenstein family
ARCTIC	19. Creature last seen here
KREMPE	20. Unfriendly professor

Frankenstein Fill In The Blank 4

_____ 1. Verdict at Justine's trial

_____ 2. Creature wanted this from humans

_____ 3. Meeting site for creature and creator

_____ 4. Frankenstein abandoned creation plans here

_____ 5. The creator

_____ 6. Creature asked for his friendship; M. De ___

_____ 7. Frankenstein compared to him

_____ 8. Subject studied by Victor

_____ 9. Creature's first feeling

_____ 10. Unfriendly professor

_____ 11. Wanted military career; _____ Frankenstein

_____ 12. Left father to marry Felix

_____ 13. Title of the book

_____ 14. Taught Safie and the creature; ___ De Lacey

_____ 15. Miserable wretch

_____ 16. Number of the creature's victims

_____ 17. Destination of letters

_____ 18. Verdict at Victor's trial

_____ 19. Friendly Irish magistrate

_____ 20. Frankenstein's best friend; ___ Clerval

Frankenstein Fill In The Blank 4 Answer Key

Answer	Clue
GUILTY	1. Verdict at Justine's trial
FRIENDSHIP	2. Creature wanted this from humans
ALPS	3. Meeting site for creature and creator
SCOTLAND	4. Frankenstein abandoned creation plans here
VICTOR	5. The creator
LACEY	6. Creature asked for his friendship; M. De ___
PROMETHEUS	7. Frankenstein compared to him
CHEMISTRY	8. Subject studied by Victor
CONFUSION	9. Creature's first feeling
KREMPE	10. Unfriendly professor
ERNEST	11. Wanted military career; _____ Frankenstein
SAFIE	12. Left father to marry Felix
FRANKENSTEIN	13. Title of the book
FELIX	14. Taught Safie and the creature; ___ De Lacey
CREATURE	15. Miserable wretch
THREE	16. Number of the creature's victims
ENGLAND	17. Destination of letters
INNOCENT	18. Verdict at Victor's trial
KIRWIN	19. Friendly Irish magistrate
HENRY	20. Frankenstein's best friend; ___ Clerval

Frankenstein Matching 1

___ 1. DISGUST
___ 2. GUILTY
___ 3. REMORSE
___ 4. OBSERVATION
___ 5. PROMETHEUS
___ 6. ALPS
___ 7. PERCY
___ 8. LETTERS
___ 9. HENRY
___ 10. WALDMAN
___ 11. GENEVA
___ 12. ELIZABETH
___ 13. WILLIAM
___ 14. SAFIE
___ 15. VICTOR
___ 16. CREATURE
___ 17. KREMPE
___ 18. READ
___ 19. LOCKET
___ 20. WALTON
___ 21. FOOD
___ 22. LIGHT
___ 23. ALPHONSE
___ 24. THREE
___ 25. CONFUSION

A. First victim; _____ Frankenstein
B. Introduced Victor to natural philosophy
C. Unfriendly professor
D. What Felix taught creature to do
E. Meeting site for creature and creator
F. Number of the creature's victims
G. Died of grief
H. The creator
I. His discussions influenced his wife
J. Rescued Frankenstein; Robert _____
K. Incriminating evidence
L. Left father to marry Felix
M. How creature learned about humans
N. Frankenstein's feeling about Justine
O. Intended for Margaret Saville
P. Uncomfortable for creature at first
Q. Creature's first feeling
R. Miserable wretch
S. Hard for creature to find
T. Verdict at Justine's trial
U. Married Victor; ___ Lavenza
V. Home of Frankenstein family
W. Frankenstein's best friend; ___ Clerval
X. Frankenstein's feeling after the creation
Y. Frankenstein compared to him

Frankenstein Matching 1 Answer Key

X - 1. DISGUST	A.	First victim; _____ Frankenstein
T - 2. GUILTY	B.	Introduced Victor to natural philosophy
N - 3. REMORSE	C.	Unfriendly professor
M - 4. OBSERVATION	D.	What Felix taught creature to do
Y - 5. PROMETHEUS	E.	Meeting site for creature and creator
E - 6. ALPS	F.	Number of the creature's victims
I - 7. PERCY	G.	Died of grief
O - 8. LETTERS	H.	The creator
W - 9. HENRY	I.	His discussions influenced his wife
B - 10. WALDMAN	J.	Rescued Frankenstein; Robert ____
V - 11. GENEVA	K.	Incriminating evidence
U - 12. ELIZABETH	L.	Left father to marry Felix
A - 13. WILLIAM	M.	How creature learned about humans
L - 14. SAFIE	N.	Frankenstein's feeling about Justine
H - 15. VICTOR	O.	Intended for Margaret Saville
R - 16. CREATURE	P.	Uncomfortable for creature at first
C - 17. KREMPE	Q.	Creature's first feeling
D - 18. READ	R.	Miserable wretch
K - 19. LOCKET	S.	Hard for creature to find
J - 20. WALTON	T.	Verdict at Justine's trial
S - 21. FOOD	U.	Married Victor; ____ Lavenza
P - 22. LIGHT	V.	Home of Frankenstein family
G - 23. ALPHONSE	W.	Frankenstein's best friend; ____ Clerval
F - 24. THREE	X.	Frankenstein's feeling after the creation
Q - 25. CONFUSION	Y.	Frankenstein compared to him

Frankenstein Matching 2

___ 1. ELIZABETH   A. Miserable wretch
___ 2. KIRWIN   B. Number of the creature's victims
___ 3. ENGLAND   C. Uncomfortable for creature at first
___ 4. FRANKENSTEIN D. Married Victor; ___ Lavenza
___ 5. ERNEST   E. Left father to marry Felix
___ 6. FELIX   F. Destination of letters
___ 7. GUILTY   G. Meeting site for creature and creator
___ 8. CORNELIUS   H. Verdict at Justine's trial
___ 9. CREATURE   I. How creature learned about humans
___10. LIGHT   J. Frankenstein compared to him
___11. PERCY   K. Subject studied by Victor
___12. LOCKET   L. Wanted military career; _____ Frankenstein
___13. CONFUSION   M. What Felix taught creature to do
___14. OBSERVATION N. Creature's request of Frankenstein
___15. ALPS   O. Title of the book
___16. READ   P. Friendly Irish magistrate
___17. CHEMISTRY   Q. His discussions influenced his wife
___18. VICTOR   R. Unfriendly professor
___19. INGOLSTADT   S. Incriminating evidence
___20. PROMETHEUS   T. Creature's first feeling
___21. KREMPE   U. Site of original creation
___22. SAFIE   V. Influential author; ____ Agrippa
___23. THREE   W. Taught Safie and the creature; ___ De Lacey
___24. FEMALE   X. The creator
___25. REMORSE   Y. Frankenstein's feeling about Justine

Frankenstein Matching 2 Answer Key

D - 1. ELIZABETH	A.	Miserable wretch
P - 2. KIRWIN	B.	Number of the creature's victims
F - 3. ENGLAND	C.	Uncomfortable for creature at first
O - 4. FRANKENSTEIN	D.	Married Victor; ___ Lavenza
L - 5. ERNEST	E.	Left father to marry Felix
W - 6. FELIX	F.	Destination of letters
H - 7. GUILTY	G.	Meeting site for creature and creator
V - 8. CORNELIUS	H.	Verdict at Justine's trial
A - 9. CREATURE	I.	How creature learned about humans
C - 10. LIGHT	J.	Frankenstein compared to him
Q - 11. PERCY	K.	Subject studied by Victor
S - 12. LOCKET	L.	Wanted military career; _____ Frankenstein
T - 13. CONFUSION	M.	What Felix taught creature to do
I - 14. OBSERVATION	N.	Creature's request of Frankenstein
G - 15. ALPS	O.	Title of the book
M - 16. READ	P.	Friendly Irish magistrate
K - 17. CHEMISTRY	Q.	His discussions influenced his wife
X - 18. VICTOR	R.	Unfriendly professor
U - 19. INGOLSTADT	S.	Incriminating evidence
J - 20. PROMETHEUS	T.	Creature's first feeling
R - 21. KREMPE	U.	Site of original creation
E - 22. SAFIE	V.	Influential author; ____ Agrippa
B - 23. THREE	W.	Taught Safie and the creature; ___ De Lacey
N - 24. FEMALE	X.	The creator
Y - 25. REMORSE	Y.	Frankenstein's feeling about Justine

Frankenstein Matching 3

___ 1. CONFUSION A. Incriminating evidence
___ 2. DISGUST B. Frankenstein's feeling about Justine
___ 3. FEMALE C. His discussions influenced his wife
___ 4. CAROLINE D. Taught Safie and the creature; ___ De Lacey
___ 5. GUILTY E. Frankenstein matriarch; ___ Beaufort
___ 6. WALTON F. Frankenstein's feeling after the creation
___ 7. SCOTLAND G. Unfriendly professor
___ 8. CREATURE H. Friendly Irish magistrate
___ 9. ENGLAND I. Left father to marry Felix
___ 10. READ J. Creature asked for his friendship; M. De ___
___ 11. LETTERS K. Miserable wretch
___ 12. LACEY L. Intended for Margaret Saville
___ 13. REMORSE M. Creature's first feeling
___ 14. HENRY N. Influential author; ___ Agrippa
___ 15. LOCKET O. Site of original creation
___ 16. KREMPE P. Destination of letters
___ 17. CHEMISTRY Q. Rescued Frankenstein; Robert ___
___ 18. INGOLSTADT R. Verdict at Justine's trial
___ 19. SAFIE S. Proposed writing ghost stories; Lord ___
___ 20. VICTOR T. The creator
___ 21. CORNELIUS U. Creature's request of Frankenstein
___ 22. BYRON V. Frankenstein's best friend; ___ Clerval
___ 23. PERCY W. What Felix taught creature to do
___ 24. KIRWIN X. Frankenstein abandoned creation plans here
___ 25. FELIX Y. Subject studied by Victor

Frankenstein Matching 3 Answer Key

M - 1.	CONFUSION	A.	Incriminating evidence
F - 2.	DISGUST	B.	Frankenstein's feeling about Justine
U - 3.	FEMALE	C.	His discussions influenced his wife
E - 4.	CAROLINE	D.	Taught Safie and the creature; ___ De Lacey
R - 5.	GUILTY	E.	Frankenstein matriarch; ____ Beaufort
Q - 6.	WALTON	F.	Frankenstein's feeling after the creation
X - 7.	SCOTLAND	G.	Unfriendly professor
K - 8.	CREATURE	H.	Friendly Irish magistrate
P - 9.	ENGLAND	I.	Left father to marry Felix
W -10.	READ	J.	Creature asked for his friendship; M. De ___
L - 11.	LETTERS	K.	Miserable wretch
J - 12.	LACEY	L.	Intended for Margaret Saville
B -13.	REMORSE	M.	Creature's first feeling
V -14.	HENRY	N.	Influential author; ____ Agrippa
A -15.	LOCKET	O.	Site of original creation
G -16.	KREMPE	P.	Destination of letters
Y -17.	CHEMISTRY	Q.	Rescued Frankenstein; Robert ____
O -18.	INGOLSTADT	R.	Verdict at Justine's trial
I - 19.	SAFIE	S.	Proposed writing ghost stories; Lord ___
T -20.	VICTOR	T.	The creator
N -21.	CORNELIUS	U.	Creature's request of Frankenstein
S -22.	BYRON	V.	Frankenstein's best friend; ___ Clerval
C -23.	PERCY	W.	What Felix taught creature to do
H -24.	KIRWIN	X.	Frankenstein abandoned creation plans here
D -25.	FELIX	Y.	Subject studied by Victor

Frankenstein Matching 4

___ 1. SAFIE A. Intended for Margaret Saville
___ 2. FOOD B. Frankenstein matriarch; ____ Beaufort
___ 3. DISGUST C. What Frankenstein wanted to create
___ 4. SCOTLAND D. Introduced Victor to natural philosophy
___ 5. PERCY E. Proposed writing ghost stories; Lord ___
___ 6. THREE F. Creature's request of Frankenstein
___ 7. ALPS G. Rescued Frankenstein; Robert ____
___ 8. CHEMISTRY H. Frankenstein's feeling after the creation
___ 9. ALPHONSE I. Destination of letters
___ 10. LACEY J. Meeting site for creature and creator
___ 11. LIFE K. His discussions influenced his wife
___ 12. MORITZ L. Wrongly executed; Justine ___
___ 13. FEMALE M. Number of the creature's victims
___ 14. BYRON N. Died of grief
___ 15. KIRWIN O. Frankenstein's feeling about Justine
___ 16. CAROLINE P. Left father to marry Felix
___ 17. GUILTY Q. How creature learned about humans
___ 18. HENRY R. Subject studied by Victor
___ 19. CORNELIUS S. Influential author; ____ Agrippa
___ 20. REMORSE T. Frankenstein's best friend; ___ Clerval
___ 21. OBSERVATION U. Frankenstein abandoned creation plans here
___ 22. ENGLAND V. Friendly Irish magistrate
___ 23. LETTERS W. Hard for creature to find
___ 24. WALDMAN X. Verdict at Justine's trial
___ 25. WALTON Y. Creature asked for his friendship; M. De ___

Frankenstein Matching 4 Answer Key

P - 1. SAFIE	A.	Intended for Margaret Saville
W - 2. FOOD	B.	Frankenstein matriarch; ____ Beaufort
H - 3. DISGUST	C.	What Frankenstein wanted to create
U - 4. SCOTLAND	D.	Introduced Victor to natural philosophy
K - 5. PERCY	E.	Proposed writing ghost stories; Lord ___
M - 6. THREE	F.	Creature's request of Frankenstein
J - 7. ALPS	G.	Rescued Frankenstein; Robert ____
R - 8. CHEMISTRY	H.	Frankenstein's feeling after the creation
N - 9. ALPHONSE	I.	Destination of letters
Y - 10. LACEY	J.	Meeting site for creature and creator
C - 11. LIFE	K.	His discussions influenced his wife
L - 12. MORITZ	L.	Wrongly executed; Justine ___
F - 13. FEMALE	M.	Number of the creature's victims
E - 14. BYRON	N.	Died of grief
V - 15. KIRWIN	O.	Frankenstein's feeling about Justine
B - 16. CAROLINE	P.	Left father to marry Felix
X - 17. GUILTY	Q.	How creature learned about humans
T - 18. HENRY	R.	Subject studied by Victor
S - 19. CORNELIUS	S.	Influential author; ____ Agrippa
O - 20. REMORSE	T.	Frankenstein's best friend; ___ Clerval
Q - 21. OBSERVATION	U.	Frankenstein abandoned creation plans here
I - 22. ENGLAND	V.	Friendly Irish magistrate
A - 23. LETTERS	W.	Hard for creature to find
D - 24. WALDMAN	X.	Verdict at Justine's trial
G - 25. WALTON	Y.	Creature asked for his friendship; M. De ___

Frankenstein Magic Squares 1

Match the definition with the vocabulary word. Put your answers in the magic squares below. When your answers are correct, all columns and rows will add to the same number.

A. BYRON
B. CREATURE
C. LOCKET
D. THREE
E. CONFUSION
F. GUILTY
G. FRANKENSTEIN
H. ELIZABETH
I. WILLIAM
J. LIFE
K. SCOTLAND
L. VICTOR
M. REMORSE
N. MORITZ
O. HENRY
P. LIGHT

1. Verdict at Justine's trial
2. First victim; _____ Frankenstein
3. Frankenstein's best friend; ___ Clerval
4. Number of the creature's victims
5. Frankenstein's feeling about Justine
6. Miserable wretch
7. Married Victor; ___ Lavenza
8. Frankenstein abandoned creation plans here
9. Incriminating evidence
10. Uncomfortable for creature at first
11. What Frankenstein wanted to create
12. Creature's first feeling
13. The creator
14. Title of the book
15. Proposed writing ghost stories; Lord ___
16. Wrongly executed; Justine ___

A=	B=	C=	D=
E=	F=	G=	H=
I=	J=	K=	L=
M=	N=	O=	P=

Frankenstein Magic Squares 1 Answer Key

Match the definition with the vocabulary word. Put your answers in the magic squares below. When your answers are correct, all columns and rows will add to the same number.

A. BYRON
B. CREATURE
C. LOCKET
D. THREE
E. CONFUSION
F. GUILTY
G. FRANKENSTEIN
H. ELIZABETH
I. WILLIAM
J. LIFE
K. SCOTLAND
L. VICTOR
M. REMORSE
N. MORITZ
O. HENRY
P. LIGHT

1. Verdict at Justine's trial
2. First victim; _____ Frankenstein
3. Frankenstein's best friend; ___ Clerval
4. Number of the creature's victims
5. Frankenstein's feeling about Justine
6. Miserable wretch
7. Married Victor; ___ Lavenza
8. Frankenstein abandoned creation plans here
9. Incriminating evidence
10. Uncomfortable for creature at first
11. What Frankenstein wanted to create
12. Creature's first feeling
13. The creator
14. Title of the book
15. Proposed writing ghost stories; Lord ___
16. Wrongly executed; Justine ___

A=15	B=6	C=9	D=4
E=12	F=1	G=14	H=7
I=2	J=11	K=8	L=13
M=5	N=16	O=3	P=10

Frankenstein Magic Squares 2

Match the definition with the vocabulary word. Put your answers in the magic squares below. When your answers are correct, all columns and rows will add to the same number.

A. PROMETHEUS   E. ENGLAND   I. KIRWIN   M. CREATURE
B. HENRY   F. INNOCENT   J. SCARLET   N. GENEVA
C. MORITZ   G. LIGHT   K. SCOTLAND   O. SAFIE
D. WALTON   H. FRIENDSHIP L. ARCTIC   P. FEMALE

1. Miserable wretch
2. Verdict at Victor's trial
3. Creature wanted this from humans
4. Left father to marry Felix
5. Creature last seen here
6. Wrongly executed; Justine ___
7. Frankenstein compared to him
8. Killed Victor's mother; ____ fever
9. Frankenstein abandoned creation plans here
10. Rescued Frankenstein; Robert ____
11. Frankenstein's best friend; ___ Clerval
12. Friendly Irish magistrate
13. Home of Frankenstein family
14. Destination of letters
15. Uncomfortable for creature at first
16. Creature's request of Frankenstein

A=	B=	C=	D=
E=	F=	G=	H=
I=	J=	K=	L=
M=	N=	O=	P=

Frankenstein Magic Squares 2 Answer Key

Match the definition with the vocabulary word. Put your answers in the magic squares below. When your answers are correct, all columns and rows will add to the same number.

A. PROMETHEUS E. ENGLAND   I. KIRWIN   M. CREATURE
B. HENRY   F. INNOCENT   J. SCARLET   N. GENEVA
C. MORITZ   G. LIGHT   K. SCOTLAND   O. SAFIE
D. WALTON   H. FRIENDSHIP L. ARCTIC   P. FEMALE

1. Miserable wretch
2. Verdict at Victor's trial
3. Creature wanted this from humans
4. Left father to marry Felix
5. Creature last seen here
6. Wrongly executed; Justine ___
7. Frankenstein compared to him
8. Killed Victor's mother; ____ fever
9. Frankenstein abandoned creation plans here
10. Rescued Frankenstein; Robert ____
11. Frankenstein's best friend; ___ Clerval
12. Friendly Irish magistrate
13. Home of Frankenstein family
14. Destination of letters
15. Uncomfortable for creature at first
16. Creature's request of Frankenstein

A=7	B=11	C=6	D=10
E=14	F=2	G=15	H=3
I=12	J=8	K=9	L=5
M=1	N=13	O=4	P=16

Frankenstein Magic Squares 3

Match the definition with the vocabulary word. Put your answers in the magic squares below. When your answers are correct, all columns and rows will add to the same number.

A. THREE
B. ARCTIC
C. SAFIE
D. WILLIAM
E. READ
F. ELIZABETH
G. ALPHONSE
H. WALTON
I. PERCY
J. MORITZ
K. DISGUST
L. SCARLET
M. ENGLAND
N. BYRON
O. FOOD
P. LIFE

1. Rescued Frankenstein; Robert _____
2. Number of the creature's victims
3. Creature last seen here
4. Died of grief
5. Wrongly executed; Justine ___
6. Hard for creature to find
7. What Frankenstein wanted to create
8. His discussions influenced his wife
9. Frankenstein's feeling after the creation
10. Proposed writing ghost stories; Lord ___
11. Destination of letters
12. Killed Victor's mother; _____ fever
13. What Felix taught creature to do
14. First victim; _____ Frankenstein
15. Left father to marry Felix
16. Married Victor; ___ Lavenza

A=	B=	C=	D=
E=	F=	G=	H=
I=	J=	K=	L=
M=	N=	O=	P=

25
Copyrighted

Frankenstein Magic Squares 3 Answer Key

Match the definition with the vocabulary word. Put your answers in the magic squares below. When your answers are correct, all columns and rows will add to the same number.

A. THREE
B. ARCTIC
C. SAFIE
D. WILLIAM
E. READ
F. ELIZABETH
G. ALPHONSE
H. WALTON
I. PERCY
J. MORITZ
K. DISGUST
L. SCARLET
M. ENGLAND
N. BYRON
O. FOOD
P. LIFE

1. Rescued Frankenstein; Robert _____
2. Number of the creature's victims
3. Creature last seen here
4. Died of grief
5. Wrongly executed; Justine ___
6. Hard for creature to find
7. What Frankenstein wanted to create
8. His discussions influenced his wife
9. Frankenstein's feeling after the creation
10. Proposed writing ghost stories; Lord ___
11. Destination of letters
12. Killed Victor's mother; _____ fever
13. What Felix taught creature to do
14. First victim; _____ Frankenstein
15. Left father to marry Felix
16. Married Victor; ___ Lavenza

A=2	B=3	C=15	D=14
E=13	F=16	G=4	H=1
I=8	J=5	K=9	L=12
M=11	N=10	O=6	P=7

Frankenstein Magic Squares 4

Match the definition with the vocabulary word. Put your answers in the magic squares below. When your answers are correct, all columns and rows will add to the same number.

A. SCARLET
B. WALTON
C. THREE
D. VICTOR
E. GUILTY
F. FOOD
G. LOCKET
H. ENGLAND
I. FELIX
J. INNOCENT
K. ARCTIC
L. CONFUSION
M. ALPS
N. MARY
O. CAROLINE
P. SCOTLAND

1. Frankenstein matriarch; ____ Beaufort
2. Verdict at Victor's trial
3. Destination of letters
4. Killed Victor's mother; ____ fever
5. The creator
6. Verdict at Justine's trial
7. Creature last seen here
8. Author of Frankenstein; ____ Shelley
9. Hard for creature to find
10. Number of the creature's victims
11. Meeting site for creature and creator
12. Creature's first feeling
13. Taught Safie and the creature; ____ De Lacey
14. Frankenstein abandoned creation plans here
15. Rescued Frankenstein; Robert ____
16. Incriminating evidence

A=	B=	C=	D=
E=	F=	G=	H=
I=	J=	K=	L=
M=	N=	O=	P=

Frankenstein Magic Squares 4 Answer Key

Match the definition with the vocabulary word. Put your answers in the magic squares below. When your answers are correct, all columns and rows will add to the same number.

A. SCARLET   E. GUILTY   I. FELIX   M. ALPS
B. WALTON   F. FOOD   J. INNOCENT   N. MARY
C. THREE   G. LOCKET   K. ARCTIC   O. CAROLINE
D. VICTOR   H. ENGLAND   L. CONFUSION   P. SCOTLAND

1. Frankenstein matriarch; ____ Beaufort
2. Verdict at Victor's trial
3. Destination of letters
4. Killed Victor's mother; ____ fever
5. The creator
6. Verdict at Justine's trial
7. Creature last seen here
8. Author of Frankenstein; ___ Shelley
9. Hard for creature to find
10. Number of the creature's victims
11. Meeting site for creature and creator
12. Creature's first feeling
13. Taught Safie and the creature; ___ De Lacey
14. Frankenstein abandoned creation plans here
15. Rescued Frankenstein; Robert ____
16. Incriminating evidence

A=4	B=15	C=10	D=5
E=6	F=9	G=16	H=3
I=13	J=2	K=7	L=12
M=11	N=8	O=1	P=14

Frankenstein Word Search 1

```
A D I S G U S T L E T T E R S T G W F Y
L S U I L E N R O C J B Z G E R X A R K
P C W D K X X S B T N C P L L X H L A L
H D N A L T O C S Z G W R Y D M W D N V
O W W C K S G S E D Q A O E N X R M K W
N D D Y A M Z Y R V C J M D A R D A E R
S K L F R R F T V S K M E Y L T G N N J
E M I M Y K O V A Y Z I T G G Y U R S S
J R F N Q C P L T T N Z H G N Y E R T G
K R E M P E G L I G H T E F E M A L E D
C I H A I Z I R O N H N U C O H H R I D
O C R F D U O L N C E N S R C X N P N E
N I A W G M S G F V K F S C V E V H E G
F S N S I T L M A R Y E C Y S P E R C Y
U O N N A N A A W P V L T T G M H R L R
S G O D O I R Y C A P I T B L T P S O R
I H T D L C R M P E L X D Y T L P T J K
O C H L T N E D S V Y T M R S L C N S G
N Q I I E N J N S J V W O O A I N N C W
G W C H E M I S T R Y L W N V B L Q B N
```

Author of Frankenstein; ___ Shelley (4)
Creature asked for his friendship; M. De ___ (5)
Creature last seen here (6)
Creature's first feeling (9)
Creature's request of Frankenstein (6)
Destination of letters (7)
Died of grief (8)
First victim; _____ Frankenstein (7)
Frankenstein abandoned creation plans here (8)
Frankenstein compared to him (10)
Frankenstein matriarch; ____ Beaufort (8)
Frankenstein's best friend; ___ Clerval (5)
Frankenstein's feeling about Justine (7)
Frankenstein's feeling after the creation (7)
Friendly Irish magistrate (6)
Hard for creature to find (4)
His discussions influenced his wife (5)
Home of Frankenstein family (6)
How creature learned about humans (11)
Incriminating evidence (6)
Influential author; ____ Agrippa (9)
Intended for Margaret Saville (7)
Introduced Victor to natural philosophy (7)
Killed Victor's mother; ____ fever (7)

Left father to marry Felix (5)
Meeting site for creature and creator (4)
Miserable wretch (8)
Number of the creature's victims (5)
Proposed writing ghost stories; Lord ___ (5)
Rescued Frankenstein; Robert ____ (6)
Site of original creation (10)
Subject studied by Victor (9)
Taught Safie and the creature; ___ De Lacey (5)
The creator (6)
Title of the book (12)
Uncomfortable for creature at first (5)
Unfriendly professor (6)
Verdict at Justine's trial (6)
Verdict at Victor's trial (8)
Wanted military career; _____ Frankenstein (6)
What Felix taught creature to do (4)
What Frankenstein wanted to create (4)
Wrongly executed; Justine ___ (6)

Frankenstein Word Search 1 Answer Key

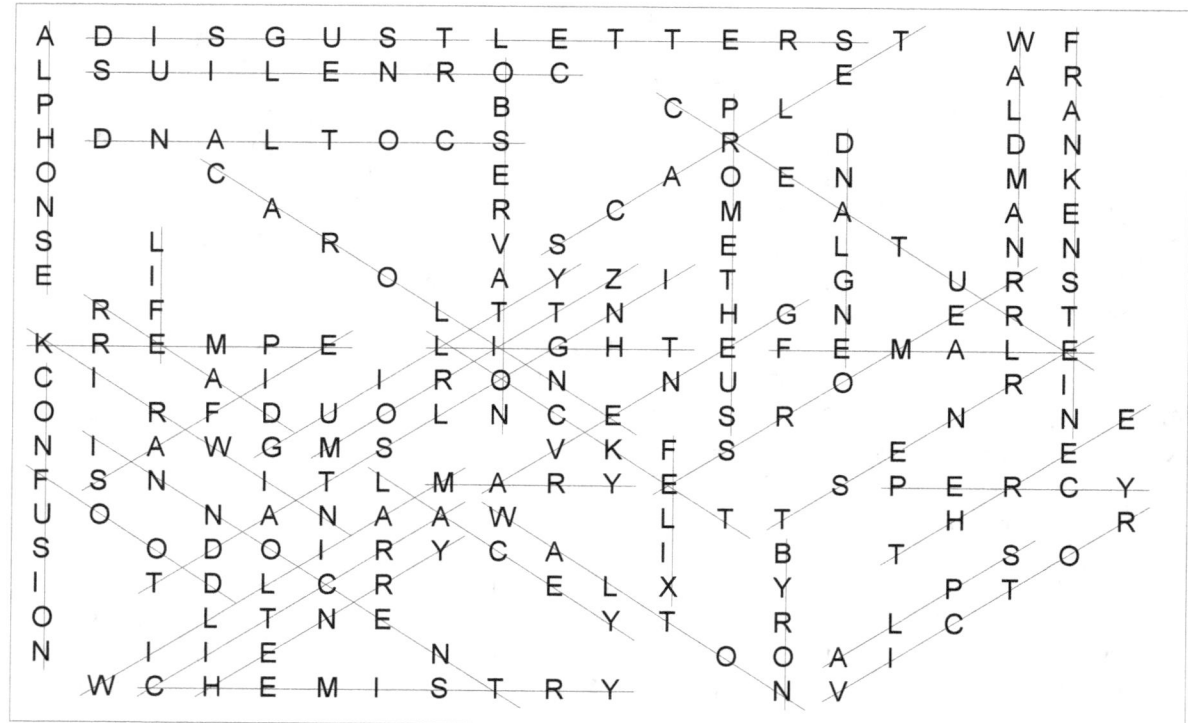

Author of Frankenstein; ___ Shelley (4)
Creature asked for his friendship; M. De ___ (5)
Creature last seen here (6)
Creature's first feeling (9)
Creature's request of Frankenstein (6)
Destination of letters (7)
Died of grief (8)
First victim; _____ Frankenstein (7)
Frankenstein abandoned creation plans here (8)
Frankenstein compared to him (10)
Frankenstein matriarch; _____ Beaufort (8)
Frankenstein's best friend; ___ Clerval (5)
Frankenstein's feeling about Justine (7)
Frankenstein's feeling after the creation (7)
Friendly Irish magistrate (6)
Hard for creature to find (4)
His discussions influenced his wife (5)
Home of Frankenstein family (6)
How creature learned about humans (11)
Incriminating evidence (6)
Influential author; ____ Agrippa (9)
Intended for Margaret Saville (7)
Introduced Victor to natural philosophy (7)
Killed Victor's mother; ____ fever (7)

Left father to marry Felix (5)
Meeting site for creature and creator (4)
Miserable wretch (8)
Number of the creature's victims (5)
Proposed writing ghost stories; Lord ___ (5)
Rescued Frankenstein; Robert ____ (6)
Site of original creation (10)
Subject studied by Victor (9)
Taught Safie and the creature; ___ De Lacey (5)
The creator (6)
Title of the book (12)
Uncomfortable for creature at first (5)
Unfriendly professor (6)
Verdict at Justine's trial (6)
Verdict at Victor's trial (8)
Wanted military career; _____ Frankenstein (6)
What Felix taught creature to do (4)
What Frankenstein wanted to create (4)
Wrongly executed; Justine ___ (6)

Frankenstein Word Search 2

```
W A L T O N K Q Z N L A S R E T T E L H
C D M N I J R X G W I L L I A M V Z O E
L O A W L M E B S Y S J G P D K R N C N
L Y R T S I M E H C O N F U S I O N K R
D I C N L Y P F O R A G W P F R T Y E Y
K D T K E Y E T R E S R P Z Y D C D T S
W Q I F E L L P M A F M L B B H I N C B
A B C C Y A I Y F T N S G E N E V A R Q
L Y A D N E C U H U O K S R T R R L E T
D L F D L R D G S R I N E B S O P G M P
M V C A E Q I B T E T F L N L Q R N O F
A Y M P C L P S L Y A B E I S S O E R W
N E L Z Z W E I Q Y V M N L F T M C S B
F M A R Y N Z D T H R E E J I E E Y E K
S K N Q R A Z I H H E E G B T X T I D P
T X L E B M G S R X S C A P L L H W N M
Y K G E L T B G K T B S D I H E H F V
C Z T I R O M U Z F O O D U C N U X G P
Y H I N G O L S T A D T G T F J S L F M
I N N O C E N T A L P H O N S E I F A S
```

Author of Frankenstein; ____ Shelley (4)
Creature asked for his friendship; M. De ____ (5)
Creature last seen here (6)
Creature's first feeling (9)
Creature's request of Frankenstein (6)
Destination of letters (7)
Died of grief (8)
First victim; _____ Frankenstein (7)
Frankenstein abandoned creation plans here (8)
Frankenstein compared to him (10)
Frankenstein matriarch; ____ Beaufort (8)
Frankenstein's best friend; ___ Clerval (5)
Frankenstein's feeling about Justine (7)
Frankenstein's feeling after the creation (7)
Friendly Irish magistrate (6)
Hard for creature to find (4)
His discussions influenced his wife (5)
Home of Frankenstein family (6)
How creature learned about humans (11)
Incriminating evidence (6)
Influential author; ____ Agrippa (9)
Intended for Margaret Saville (7)
Introduced Victor to natural philosophy (7)
Killed Victor's mother; ____ fever (7)

Left father to marry Felix (5)
Married Victor; ___ Lavenza (9)
Meeting site for creature and creator (4)
Miserable wretch (8)
Number of the creature's victims (5)
Proposed writing ghost stories; Lord ___ (5)
Rescued Frankenstein; Robert ____ (6)
Site of original creation (10)
Subject studied by Victor (9)
Taught Safie and the creature; ___ De Lacey (5)
The creator (6)
Title of the book (12)
Uncomfortable for creature at first (5)
Unfriendly professor (6)
Verdict at Justine's trial (6)
Verdict at Victor's trial (8)
Wanted military career; _____ Frankenstein (6)
What Felix taught creature to do (4)
What Frankenstein wanted to create (4)
Wrongly executed; Justine ___ (6)

Frankenstein Word Search 2 Answer Key

```
W  A  L  T  O  N     K                          A  S  R  E  T  T  E  L     H
C              I     R              W  I  L  L  I  A  M              O     E
   O  A  W           E        S     S              P        R  N     C     N
   Y  R  T  S  I  M  E  H  C  O  N  F  U  S  I  O  N     K           R
      I  C  N        P  F  O  R  A              R        T        E        Y
   K     T     E  Y  E  T  R  E     R        Y        C  D        T
   W        I     E  L  L     A     L  B           I  N           C
   A        C  C     A  I  Y     T        G  E  N  E  V  A        R
      L     A     N  E  C  U  H  U  O  K        T     R  L        E
   D        D  L     R  G  S  R  I        E        O  P  G        M
   M           A  E     I     T  E  T  F  L  N     R  N           O
   A              M  P  L     S  L     A  E  I  S  O  E           R
   N  E                 E     I        V  N  L  F  T  M           S
   F  M  A  R  Y     N  Z  D  T  H  R  E  E     I  E  Y           E
               R  A        I           E  E     X     T     I
               E  B        S           E     A        L  H     N
                  E        G           B        D     E
         Z  T  I     R  O  M  U        F  O  O  D  U  U
         H  I  N  G  O  L  S  T  A  D  T     G        S
         I  N  N  O  C  E  N  T  A  L  P  H  O  N  S  E  I  F  A  S
```

Author of Frankenstein; ___ Shelley (4)
Creature asked for his friendship; M. De ___ (5)
Creature last seen here (6)
Creature's first feeling (9)
Creature's request of Frankenstein (6)
Destination of letters (7)
Died of grief (8)
First victim; _____ Frankenstein (7)
Frankenstein abandoned creation plans here (8)
Frankenstein compared to him (10)
Frankenstein matriarch; ____ Beaufort (8)
Frankenstein's best friend; ___ Clerval (5)
Frankenstein's feeling about Justine (7)
Frankenstein's feeling after the creation (7)
Friendly Irish magistrate (6)
Hard for creature to find (4)
His discussions influenced his wife (5)
Home of Frankenstein family (6)
How creature learned about humans (11)
Incriminating evidence (6)
Influential author; ____ Agrippa (9)
Intended for Margaret Saville (7)
Introduced Victor to natural philosophy (7)
Killed Victor's mother; ____ fever (7)

Left father to marry Felix (5)
Married Victor; ___ Lavenza (9)
Meeting site for creature and creator (4)
Miserable wretch (8)
Number of the creature's victims (5)
Proposed writing ghost stories; Lord ___ (5)
Rescued Frankenstein; Robert ____ (6)
Site of original creation (10)
Subject studied by Victor (9)
Taught Safie and the creature; ___ De Lacey (5)
The creator (6)
Title of the book (12)
Uncomfortable for creature at first (5)
Unfriendly professor (6)
Verdict at Justine's trial (6)
Verdict at Victor's trial (8)
Wanted military career; _____ Frankenstein (6)
What Felix taught creature to do (4)
What Frankenstein wanted to create (4)
Wrongly executed; Justine ___ (6)

Copyrighted

Frankenstein Word Search 3

```
K P X V K C D Y Y R C Y A D M L S F V G
L K Z Q R R B R C Q Z R V P Y H W J S H
P I H S D N E I R F S N E D T M B N J E
P L X H J F Y M E V C N C L L A C E Z
F O O D R Y A L P S C H E M I S T R Y D
L E P K O R W T E E E L G G U M H E Y L
C O L N G B S A B T A L H T G T T A K P
L R C I H N S Z L M T T I D A R C T I C
V Z A K X Y U E E T W E N Z V T E U R N
C Y R H E B I F R X O A R F A L F R W M
N Z O Y W T L R D V L N W S R B W E I W
Q L L I S P E G E G A Z P A Z L E X N G
V N I E N A N G N M M T C T L S A T N V
W P N F D N R E H F O S I V J D A C H C
D R E D E P O G P N V R J O S V M F E F
E I N V R V C C O R O N S F N I G A I Y
S J S Y C X T I E M O M N E L C M X N E
N V K G W G S J C N B M B F E T H K G V
R K W F U U C G C O T P E S G O G M O H
F Z W V F S O R N R X S N T Y R A K L N
J H K N L G T G X Y F O P F H I Y T S K
N N O T Z N L S H B H Q F L L E P Q T K
F C W R R Y A J D P T Z Q L Q N U M A M
R J P S G B N N L S B J I S V M D S D R
T Y C B G V D A M X T W C C V G S Y T S
```

ALPHONSE	DISGUST	GUILTY	LIGHT	SAFIE
ALPS	ELIZABETH	HENRY	LOCKET	SCARLET
ARCTIC	ENGLAND	INGOLSTADT	MARY	SCOTLAND
BYRON	ERNEST	INNOCENT	MORITZ	THREE
CAROLINE	FELIX	KIRWIN	OBSERVATION	VICTOR
CHEMISTRY	FEMALE	KREMPE	PERCY	WALDMAN
CONFUSION	FOOD	LACEY	PROMETHEUS	WALTON
CORNELIUS	FRIENDSHIP	LETTERS	READ	WILLIAM
CREATURE	GENEVA	LIFE	REMORSE	

Frankenstein Word Search 3

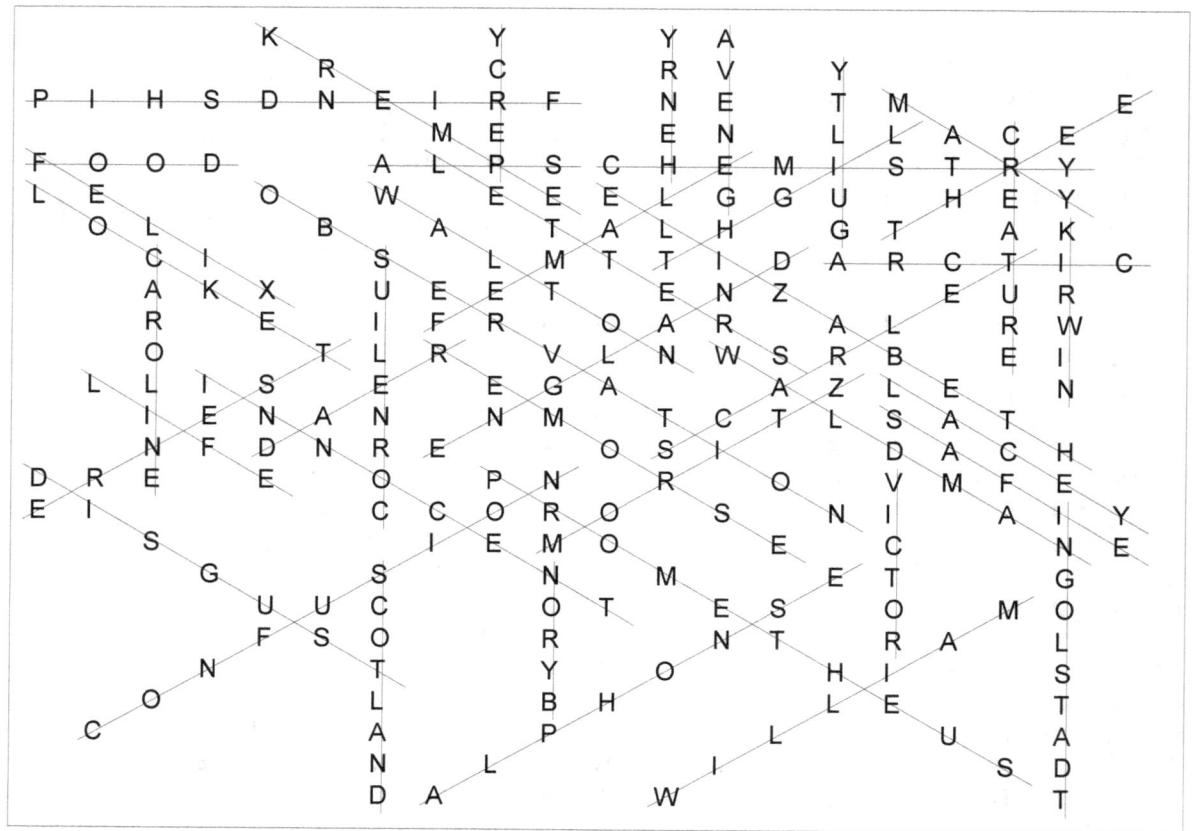

ALPHONSE	DISGUST	GUILTY	LIGHT	SAFIE
ALPS	ELIZABETH	HENRY	LOCKET	SCARLET
ARCTIC	ENGLAND	INGOLSTADT	MARY	SCOTLAND
BYRON	ERNEST	INNOCENT	MORITZ	THREE
CAROLINE	FELIX	KIRWIN	OBSERVATION	VICTOR
CHEMISTRY	FEMALE	KREMPE	PERCY	WALDMAN
CONFUSION	FOOD	LACEY	PROMETHEUS	WALTON
CORNELIUS	FRIENDSHIP	LETTERS	READ	WILLIAM
CREATURE	GENEVA	LIFE	REMORSE	

Frankenstein Word Search 4

```
E J T E L R A C S F E L I X W D I R Z D
D R M V L A V W S G Q Q X K A I N E Y Q
Q X N G J I L R A F T G L I L S N A C K
F B N F L M Q Z P J L B R X R D G O D X K
F R R S N F A H Z T J J W M U C B S J
X J I W G T K S B O J O M I A S E L C R
M Z E P L L C M T E N N N N T N H C H
H E N R Y F N H D R T S F H E C T G G S
J B D K Q L O L D K H H E P J A S W N Q
V Y S R S Y I N L G W T M L L R F R F D
K M H Z V R T R X V X E S E R O P E V Z
Z T I F Q T A T Y K R C U T L L B M D S
F Q P S Z S V E T K X C E T X I G O N Z
C D W K X I R N V S B X H E X N K R A V
W R P Z S M E G F I D M T R N E F S L Q
I C E E Q E S L L H C R E S O Q E E T J
L X N A R H B A G K S T M M R K M D O K
L I G H T C O N F U S I O N Y R A M C J
I G X H I U Y D I L I R R B T L L S B
A H R T S C R L B W I P L S M E R P J
M E C V N F E E N T S B T L A L B C B S
E R A V E N E G Z D Q A O Y V C L I F E
A B B B R M K K O T C G F Y J Z E X J T
G P G O F G R O Y S N F P I K V Q Y R P
L O C K E T F H N I E T S N E K N A R F
```

ALPHONSE DISGUST GENEVA LIFE REMORSE

ALPS ELIZABETH GUILTY LIGHT SAFIE

ARCTIC ENGLAND HENRY LOCKET SCARLET

BYRON ERNEST INGOLSTADT MARY SCOTLAND

CAROLINE FELIX INNOCENT MORITZ THREE

CHEMISTRY FEMALE KIRWIN OBSERVATION VICTOR

CONFUSION FOOD KREMPE PERCY WALDMAN

CORNELIUS FRANKENSTEIN LACEY PROMETHEUS WALTON

CREATURE FRIENDSHIP LETTERS READ WILLIAM

MARY COLLINS

Frankenstein Word Search 4 Answer Key

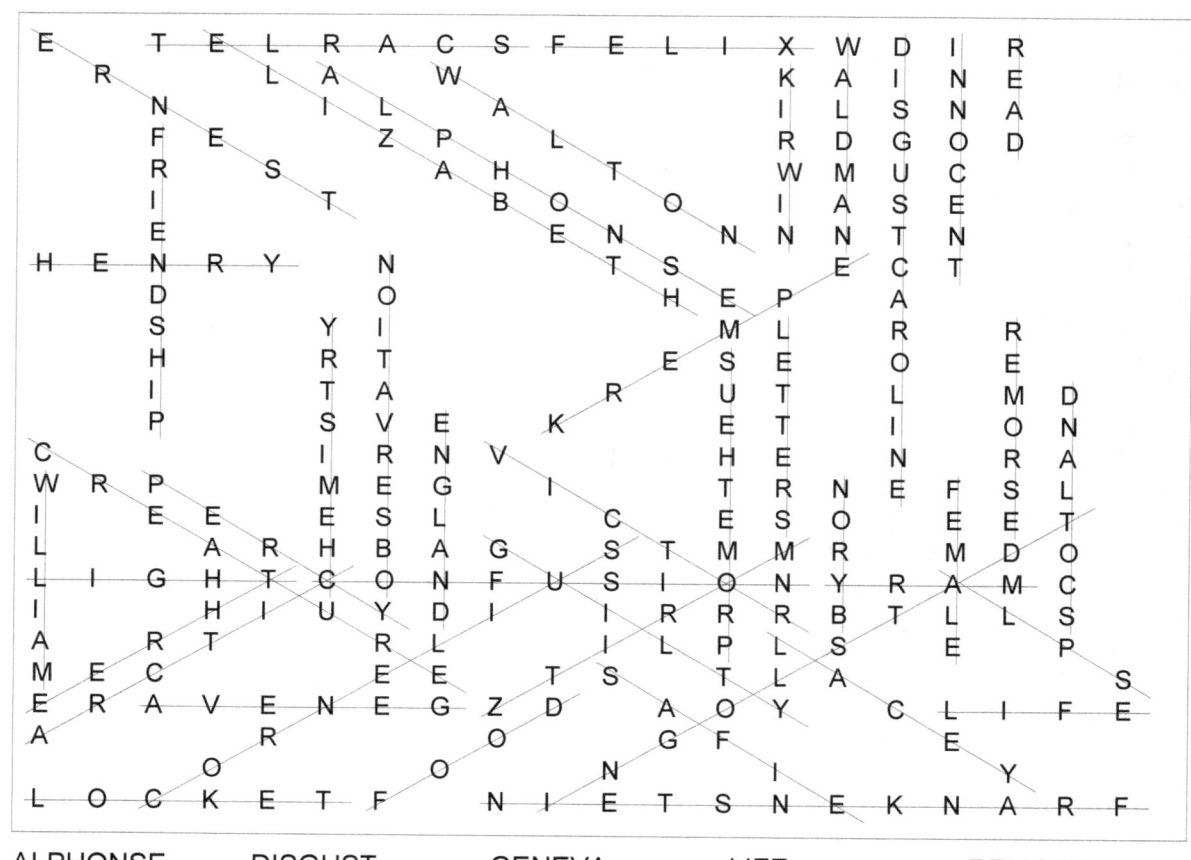

ALPHONSE	DISGUST	GENEVA	LIFE	REMORSE
ALPS	ELIZABETH	GUILTY	LIGHT	SAFIE
ARCTIC	ENGLAND	HENRY	LOCKET	SCARLET
BYRON	ERNEST	INGOLSTADT	MARY	SCOTLAND
CAROLINE	FELIX	INNOCENT	MORITZ	THREE
CHEMISTRY	FEMALE	KIRWIN	OBSERVATION	VICTOR
CONFUSION	FOOD	KREMPE	PERCY	WALDMAN
CORNELIUS	FRANKENSTEIN	LACEY	PROMETHEUS	WALTON
CREATURE	FRIENDSHIP	LETTERS	READ	WILLIAM

Frankenstein Crossword 1

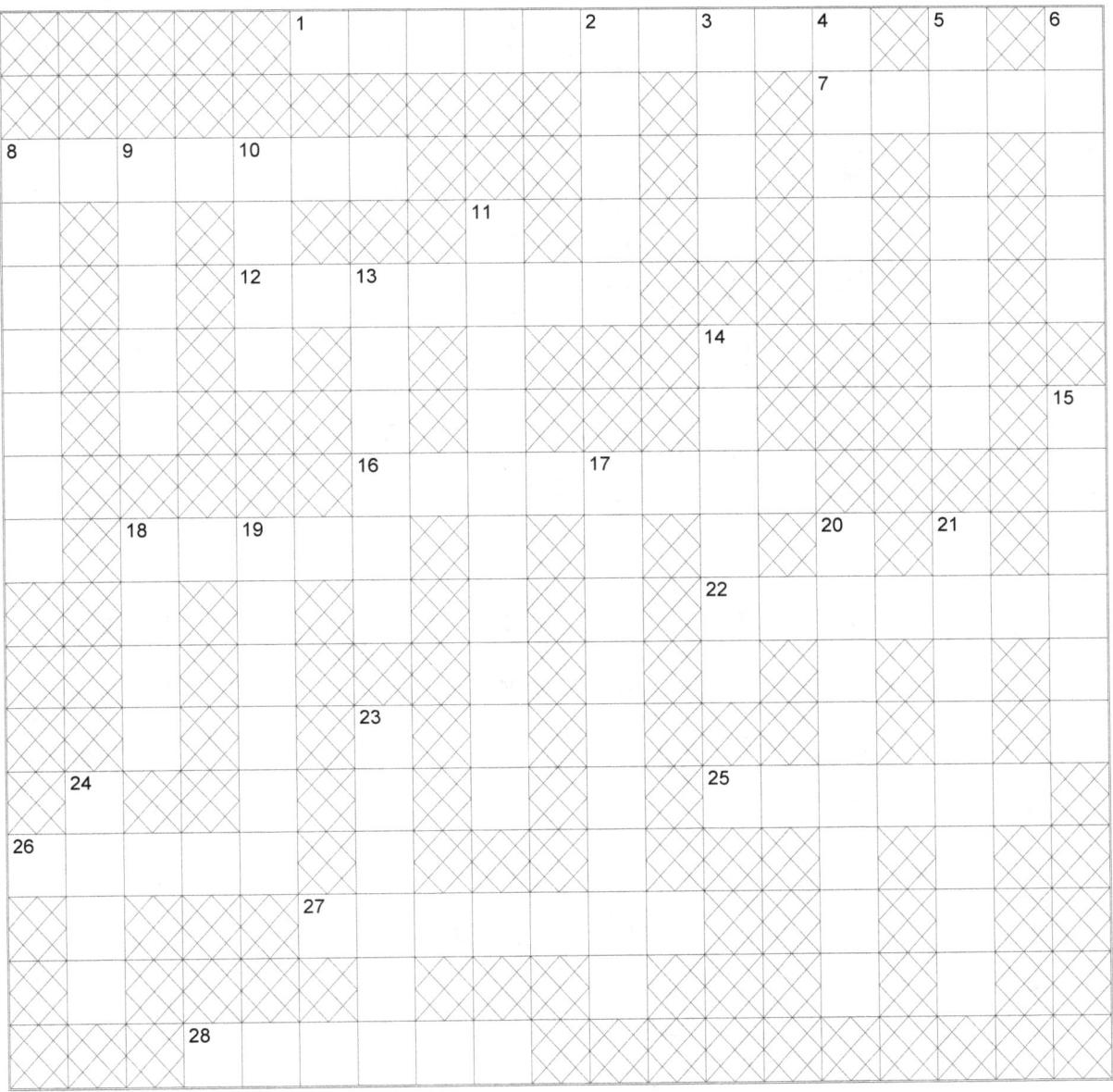

Across
1. Site of original creation
7. Frankenstein's best friend; ___ Clerval
8. Introduced Victor to natural philosophy
12. Frankenstein's feeling about Justine
16. Verdict at Victor's trial
18. Uncomfortable for creature at first
22. Killed Victor's mother; ____ fever
25. Rescued Frankenstein; Robert ____
26. His discussions influenced his wife
27. Intended for Margaret Saville
28. Creature's request of Frankenstein

Down
2. Left father to marry Felix
3. Meeting site for creature and creator
4. Number of the creature's victims
5. Destination of letters
6. Proposed writing ghost stories; Lord ___
8. First victim; _____ Frankenstein
9. Creature asked for his friendship; M. De ___
10. Author of Frankenstein; ___ Shelley
11. Creature wanted this from humans
13. Wrongly executed; Justine ___
14. Wanted military career; _____ Frankenstein
15. The creator
17. Subject studied by Victor
18. What Frankenstein wanted to create
19. Verdict at Justine's trial
20. Frankenstein matriarch; ____ Beaufort
21. Died of grief
23. Home of Frankenstein family
24. What Felix taught creature to do

Frankenstein Crossword 1 Answer Key

				1 I	N	G	O	L	2 S	T	3 A	D	4 T		5 E		6 B
									A		L		7 H	E	N	R	Y
8 W	A	9 L	10 D	M	A	N			F		P		R		G		R
I		A	A			11 F		I		S		E		L		O
L		C	12 R	E	13 M	O	R	S	E				E		A		N
L		E	Y		O		I				14 E				N	
I		Y			R		E				R				D		15 V
A					16 I	N	N	O	17 C	E	N	T					I
M		18 L	19 G	H	T		D		H		E		20 C		21 A		C
		I	U		Z		S		E		22 S	C	A	R	L	E	T
		F	I				H		M		T		R		P		O
		E	L		23 G	I		I			R		O		H		R
24 R		T	E		P	25 S	W	A	L	T	O	N			
26 P	E	R	C	Y		N			T				I		N	
		A		27 L	E	T	T	E	R	S			N		S	
		D		V				Y				E		E	
			28 F	E	M	A	L	E							

Across
1. Site of original creation
7. Frankenstein's best friend; ___ Clerval
8. Introduced Victor to natural philosophy
12. Frankenstein's feeling about Justine
16. Verdict at Victor's trial
18. Uncomfortable for creature at first
22. Killed Victor's mother; ____ fever
25. Rescued Frankenstein; Robert ____
26. His discussions influenced his wife
27. Intended for Margaret Saville
28. Creature's request of Frankenstein

Down
2. Left father to marry Felix
3. Meeting site for creature and creator
4. Number of the creature's victims
5. Destination of letters
6. Proposed writing ghost stories; Lord ___
8. First victim; _____ Frankenstein
9. Creature asked for his friendship; M. De ___
10. Author of Frankenstein; ___ Shelley
11. Creature wanted this from humans
13. Wrongly executed; Justine ___
14. Wanted military career; _____ Frankenstein
15. The creator
17. Subject studied by Victor
18. What Frankenstein wanted to create
19. Verdict at Justine's trial
20. Frankenstein matriarch; ____ Beaufort
21. Died of grief
23. Home of Frankenstein family
24. What Felix taught creature to do

Frankenstein Crossword 2

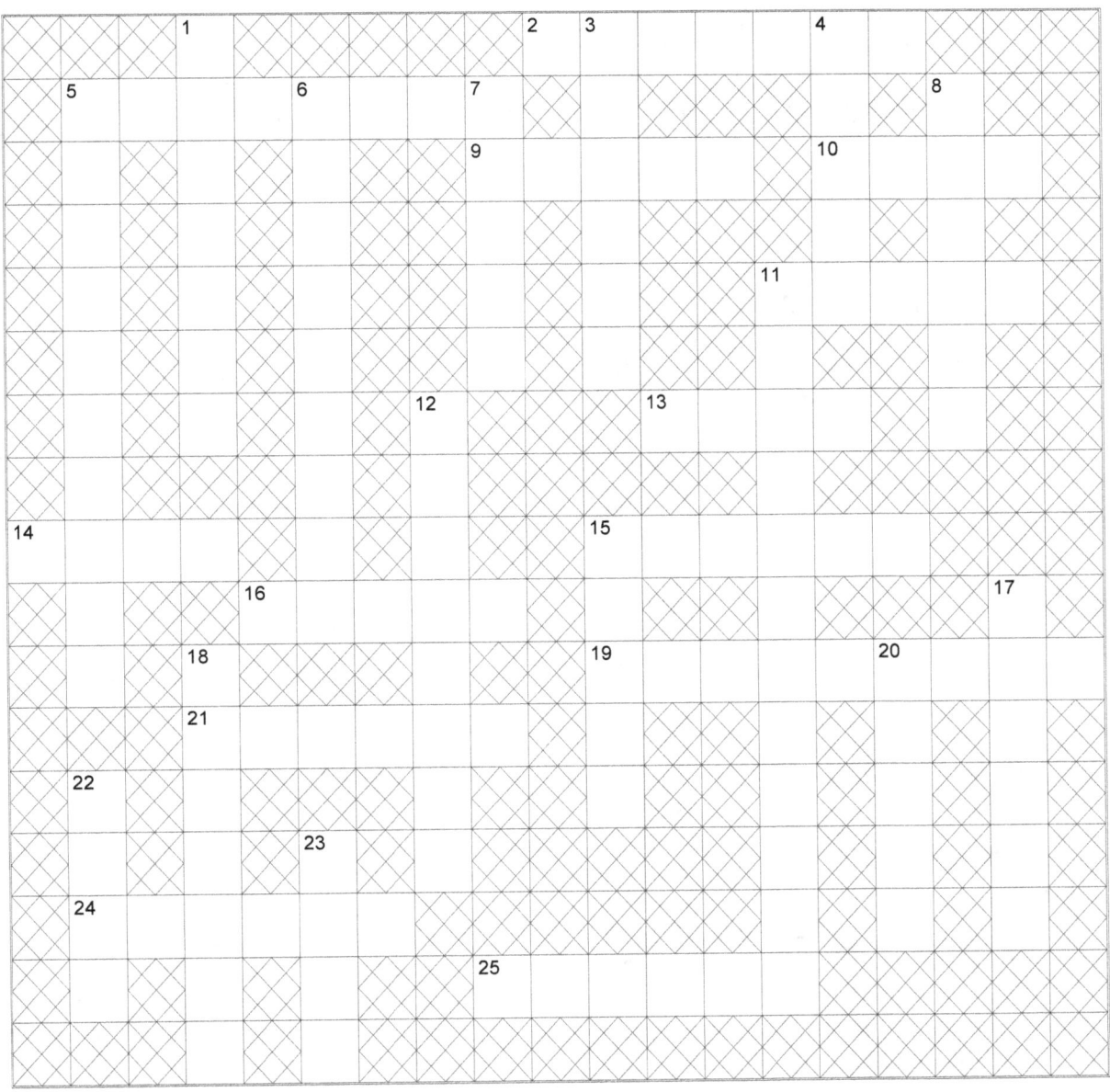

Across
2. Frankenstein's feeling about Justine
5. Verdict at Victor's trial
9. Frankenstein's best friend; ___ Clerval
10. Hard for creature to find
11. Taught Safie and the creature; ___ De Lacey
13. What Felix taught creature to do
14. Author of Frankenstein; ___ Shelley
15. Incriminating evidence
16. Proposed writing ghost stories; Lord ___
19. Influential author; ___ Agrippa
21. Creature last seen here
24. Creature's request of Frankenstein
25. Friendly Irish magistrate

Down
1. Destination of letters
3. Wanted military career; ___ Frankenstein
4. Left father to marry Felix
5. Site of original creation
6. Subject studied by Victor
7. Number of the creature's victims
8. Wrongly executed; Justine ___
11. Title of the book
12. Frankenstein matriarch; ___ Beaufort
15. Creature asked for his friendship; M. De ___
17. Verdict at Justine's trial
18. Introduced Victor to natural philosophy
20. Uncomfortable for creature at first
22. What Frankenstein wanted to create
23. Meeting site for creature and creator

Frankenstein Crossword 2 Answer Key

	1	2	3		4	
	E		R	E	M	O	R	S	E
5 I	N	N	O	6 C	E	7 N	T		R		A		8 M
	N	G		H		9 H	E	N	R	Y		10 F	O	O	D
	G	L		E			R		E			I			R
	O	A		M			E		S		11 F	E	L	I	X
	L	N		I			E		T		R				T
	S	D		S		12 C		13 R	E	A	D		Z
	T			T		A				N			
14 M	A	R	Y		R		R		15 L	O	C	K	E	T
	D		16 B	Y	R	O	N		A		E			17 G
	T		18 W			L		19 C	O	R	N	20 E	L	I	U	S
		21 A	R	C	T	I	C		E		S		I		I
22 L		L			N		Y		T		G		L
I		D	23 A		E				E		H		T
24 F	E	M	A	L	E				I		T		Y
E		A	P		25 K	I	R	W	I	N
N		S

Across
2. Frankenstein's feeling about Justine
5. Verdict at Victor's trial
9. Frankenstein's best friend; ___ Clerval
10. Hard for creature to find
11. Taught Safie and the creature; ___ De Lacey
13. What Felix taught creature to do
14. Author of Frankenstein; ___ Shelley
15. Incriminating evidence
16. Proposed writing ghost stories; Lord ___
19. Influential author; ____ Agrippa
21. Creature last seen here
24. Creature's request of Frankenstein
25. Friendly Irish magistrate

Down
1. Destination of letters
3. Wanted military career; _____ Frankenstein
4. Left father to marry Felix
5. Site of original creation
6. Subject studied by Victor
7. Number of the creature's victims
8. Wrongly executed; Justine ___
11. Title of the book
12. Frankenstein matriarch; ____ Beaufort
15. Creature asked for his friendship; M. De ___
17. Verdict at Justine's trial
18. Introduced Victor to natural philosophy
20. Uncomfortable for creature at first
22. What Frankenstein wanted to create
23. Meeting site for creature and creator

Frankenstein Crossword 3

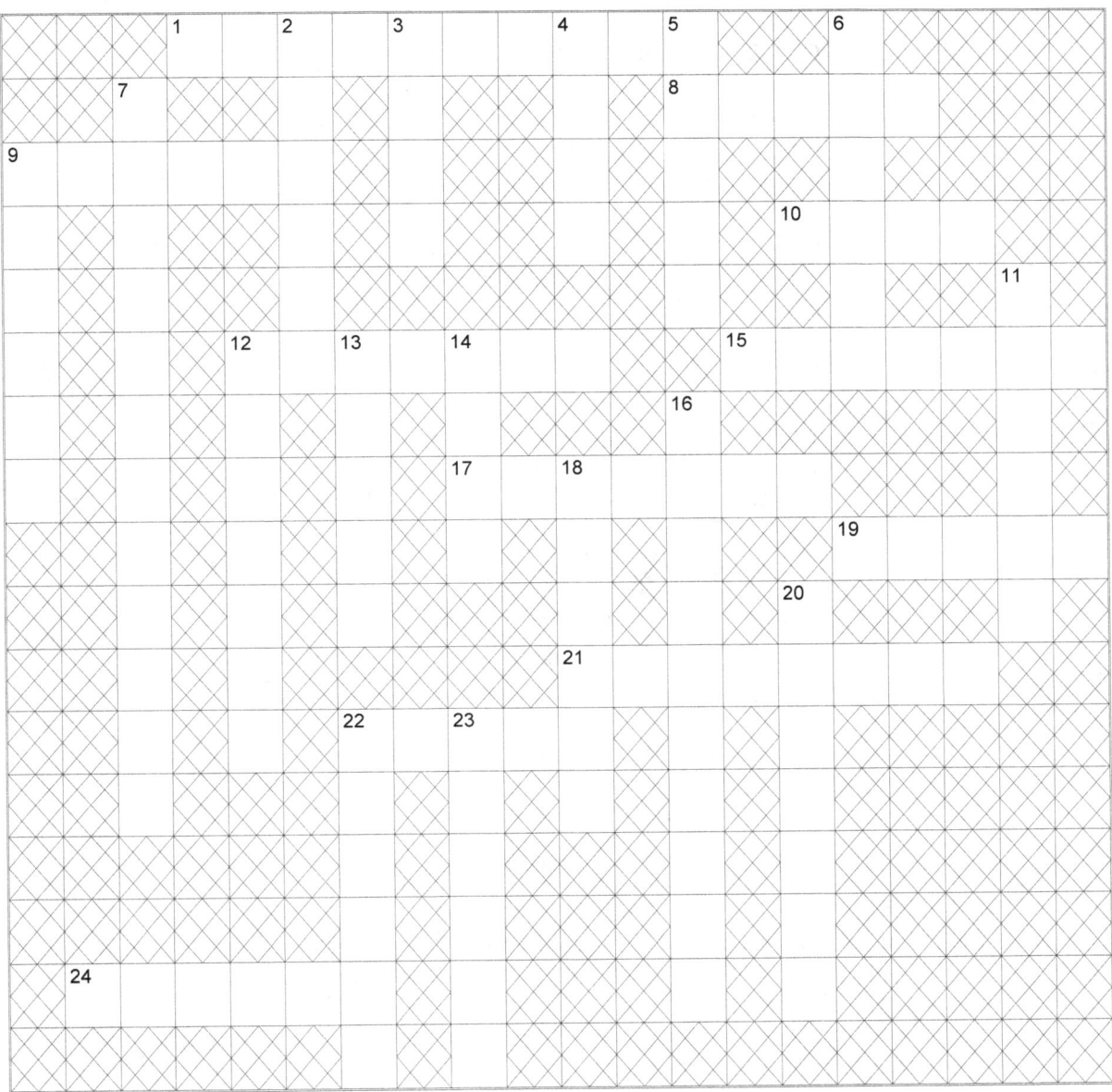

Across
1. Site of original creation
8. Frankenstein's best friend; ___ Clerval
9. Friendly Irish magistrate
10. What Felix taught creature to do
12. Introduced Victor to natural philosophy
15. Intended for Margaret Saville
17. Frankenstein's feeling about Justine
19. Left father to marry Felix
21. Verdict at Victor's trial
22. Uncomfortable for creature at first
24. Creature's request of Frankenstein

Down
2. Home of Frankenstein family
3. What Frankenstein wanted to create
4. Meeting site for creature and creator
5. Number of the creature's victims
6. Wanted military career; _____ Frankenstein
7. Title of the book
9. Unfriendly professor
11. Creature last seen here
12. First victim; _____ Frankenstein
13. Creature asked for his friendship; M. De ___
14. Author of Frankenstein; ___ Shelley
16. Creature wanted this from humans
18. Wrongly executed; Justine ___
20. Killed Victor's mother; ____ fever
22. Incriminating evidence
23. Verdict at Justine's trial

Frankenstein Crossword 3 Answer Key

		1 I	2 N	3 G	O	4 L	S	T	5 A	D	T		6 E	
	7 F		E		I		L		8 H	E	N	R	Y	
9 K	I	R	W	I	N		F		P		R		N	
R		A		E		E			S		E	10 R	E	A	D
E		N		V					E			S		11 A
M		K	12 W	A	13 L	D	14 M	A	N		15 L	E	T	T	E	R	S
P		E	I		A		A			16 F				C
E		N	L		C	17 R	E	18 M	O	R	S	E		T
		S	L		E	Y		O		I		19 S	A	F	I	E
		T	I		Y			R	E		20 S			C
		E	A				21 I	N	N	O	C	E	N	T
		I	M	22 L	23 I	G	H	T		D		A		
		N		O	U			Z		S		R		
				C	I					H		L		
				K	L					I		E		
	24 F	E	M	A	L	E		T		P		T		
				T		Y								

Across
1. Site of original creation
8. Frankenstein's best friend; ___ Clerval
9. Friendly Irish magistrate
10. What Felix taught creature to do
12. Introduced Victor to natural philosophy
15. Intended for Margaret Saville
17. Frankenstein's feeling about Justine
19. Left father to marry Felix
21. Verdict at Victor's trial
22. Uncomfortable for creature at first
24. Creature's request of Frankenstein

Down
2. Home of Frankenstein family
3. What Frankenstein wanted to create
4. Meeting site for creature and creator
5. Number of the creature's victims
6. Wanted military career; ____ Frankenstein
7. Title of the book
9. Unfriendly professor
11. Creature last seen here
12. First victim; _____ Frankenstein
13. Creature asked for his friendship; M. De ___
14. Author of Frankenstein; ___ Shelley
16. Creature wanted this from humans
18. Wrongly executed; Justine ___
20. Killed Victor's mother; ____ fever
22. Incriminating evidence
23. Verdict at Justine's trial

Frankenstein Crossword 4

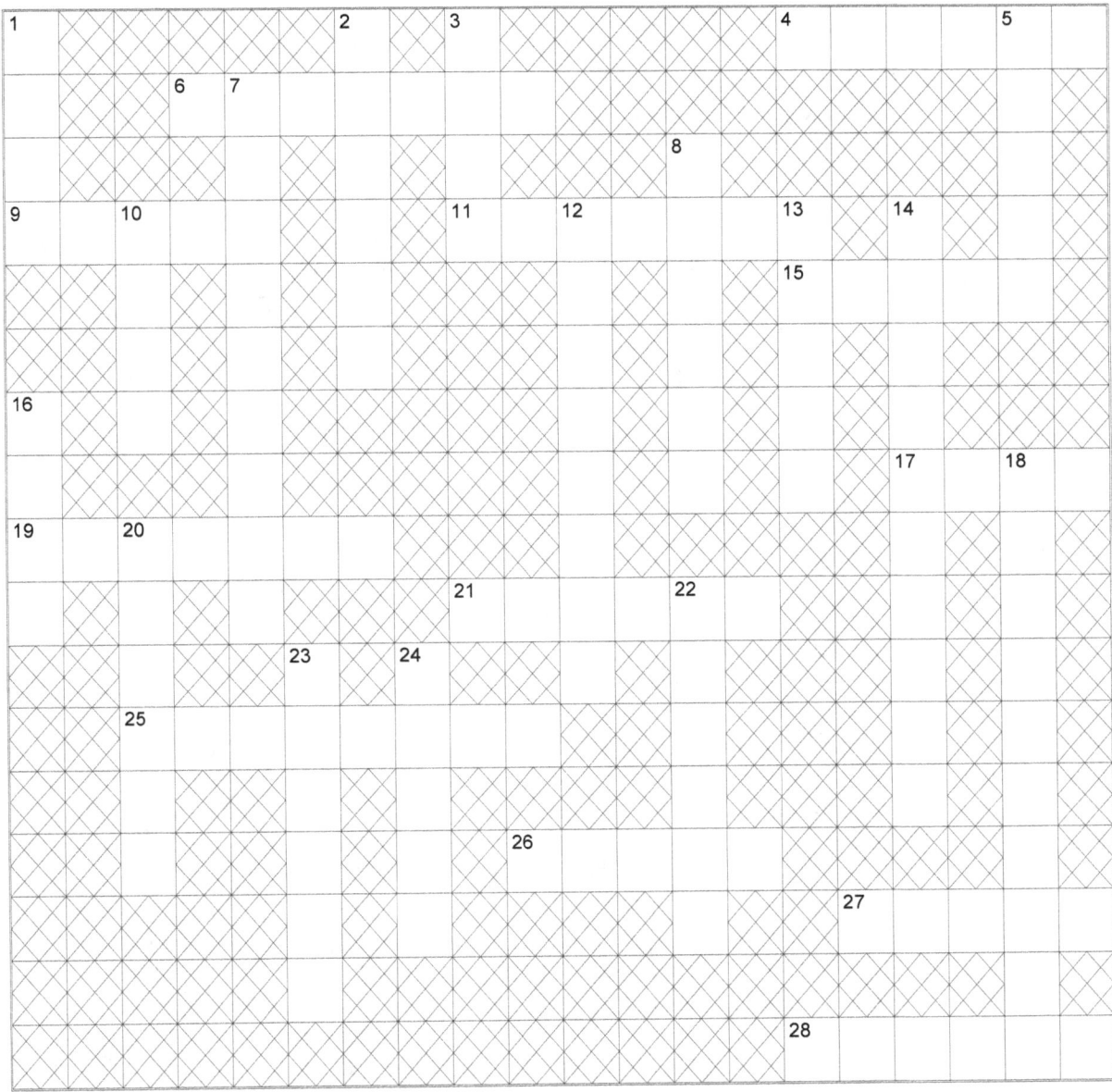

Across
4. Creature's request of Frankenstein
6. Killed Victor's mother; ____ fever
9. Left father to marry Felix
11. Frankenstein's feeling after the creation
15. Frankenstein's best friend; ___ Clerval
17. What Frankenstein wanted to create
19. Frankenstein's feeling about Justine
21. Home of Frankenstein family
25. Verdict at Victor's trial
26. Proposed writing ghost stories; Lord ___
27. Uncomfortable for creature at first
28. Unfriendly professor

Down
1. Meeting site for creature and creator
2. Wanted military career; _____ Frankenstein
3. What Felix taught creature to do
5. Creature asked for his friendship; M. De ___
7. Subject studied by Victor
8. Verdict at Justine's trial
10. Hard for creature to find
12. Frankenstein abandoned creation plans here
13. Number of the creature's victims
14. Site of original creation
16. Author of Frankenstein; ___ Shelley
18. Creature wanted this from humans
20. Wrongly executed; Justine ___
22. The creator
23. Incriminating evidence
24. His discussions influenced his wife

Frankenstein Crossword 4 Answer Key

Across
4. Creature's request of Frankenstein
6. Killed Victor's mother; ____ fever
9. Left father to marry Felix
11. Frankenstein's feeling after the creation
15. Frankenstein's best friend; ___ Clerval
17. What Frankenstein wanted to create
19. Frankenstein's feeling about Justine
21. Home of Frankenstein family
25. Verdict at Victor's trial
26. Proposed writing ghost stories; Lord ___
27. Uncomfortable for creature at first
28. Unfriendly professor

Down
1. Meeting site for creature and creator
2. Wanted military career; _____ Frankenstein
3. What Felix taught creature to do
5. Creature asked for his friendship; M. De ___
7. Subject studied by Victor
8. Verdict at Justine's trial
10. Hard for creature to find
12. Frankenstein abandoned creation plans here
13. Number of the creature's victims
14. Site of original creation
16. Author of Frankenstein; ___ Shelley
18. Creature wanted this from humans
20. Wrongly executed; Justine ___
22. The creator
23. Incriminating evidence
24. His discussions influenced his wife

Frankenstein

CONFUSION	FRIENDSHIP	OBSERVATION	ERNEST	PROMETHEUS
MARY	WALTON	READ	LOCKET	LACEY
FRANKENSTEIN	ALPS	FREE SPACE	WALDMAN	CREATURE
PERCY	GUILTY	HENRY	SAFIE	GENEVA
CHEMISTRY	CORNELIUS	LIGHT	FEMALE	FELIX

Frankenstein

FOOD	VICTOR	THREE	ALPHONSE	INGOLSTADT
KIRWIN	DISGUST	LIFE	SCOTLAND	ELIZABETH
LETTERS	REMORSE	FREE SPACE	ENGLAND	MORITZ
WILLIAM	INNOCENT	KREMPE	SCARLET	BYRON
FELIX	FEMALE	LIGHT	CORNELIUS	CHEMISTRY

Frankenstein

GUILTY	ELIZABETH	LIFE	LIGHT	FRIENDSHIP
FELIX	OBSERVATION	FRANKENSTEIN	HENRY	INGOLSTADT
LOCKET	REMORSE	FREE SPACE	CORNELIUS	INNOCENT
SCOTLAND	ENGLAND	MARY	CAROLINE	ALPS
KREMPE	READ	GENEVA	KIRWIN	PROMETHEUS

Frankenstein

CONFUSION	ARCTIC	ERNEST	DISGUST	FEMALE
FOOD	LACEY	WILLIAM	SCARLET	LETTERS
WALDMAN	CREATURE	FREE SPACE	ALPHONSE	SAFIE
BYRON	PERCY	MORITZ	THREE	CHEMISTRY
PROMETHEUS	KIRWIN	GENEVA	READ	KREMPE

Frankenstein

ALPHONSE	HENRY	CAROLINE	REMORSE	LIGHT
BYRON	LACEY	ELIZABETH	FRIENDSHIP	WALDMAN
CHEMISTRY	GUILTY	FREE SPACE	WILLIAM	VICTOR
MORITZ	GENEVA	FOOD	LIFE	ARCTIC
CREATURE	LETTERS	KREMPE	ERNEST	PERCY

Frankenstein

SAFIE	CONFUSION	FEMALE	DISGUST	WALTON
CORNELIUS	LOCKET	PROMETHEUS	ENGLAND	MARY
KIRWIN	ALPS	FREE SPACE	SCOTLAND	FELIX
FRANKENSTEIN	THREE	SCARLET	READ	INNOCENT
PERCY	ERNEST	KREMPE	LETTERS	CREATURE

Frankenstein

BYRON	LETTERS	KREMPE	LIFE	MORITZ
SAFIE	WILLIAM	INGOLSTADT	WALDMAN	DISGUST
GENEVA	CHEMISTRY	FREE SPACE	CORNELIUS	THREE
LACEY	SCOTLAND	OBSERVATION	LOCKET	ERNEST
KIRWIN	FOOD	GUILTY	CONFUSION	FRIENDSHIP

Frankenstein

CREATURE	PROMETHEUS	FELIX	INNOCENT	MARY
CAROLINE	VICTOR	REMORSE	LIGHT	ALPS
HENRY	ELIZABETH	FREE SPACE	FEMALE	ARCTIC
SCARLET	FRANKENSTEIN	ALPHONSE	PERCY	WALTON
FRIENDSHIP	CONFUSION	GUILTY	FOOD	KIRWIN

Frankenstein

LIGHT	ERNEST	ARCTIC	HENRY	FELIX
DISGUST	ELIZABETH	GENEVA	FRANKENSTEIN	WALDMAN
LOCKET	CHEMISTRY	FREE SPACE	SCARLET	KREMPE
ALPS	INGOLSTADT	SAFIE	THREE	CORNELIUS
FRIENDSHIP	KIRWIN	CONFUSION	MORITZ	ENGLAND

Frankenstein

CREATURE	ALPHONSE	FEMALE	VICTOR	LIFE
PERCY	MARY	LACEY	SCOTLAND	CAROLINE
FOOD	REMORSE	FREE SPACE	WILLIAM	WALTON
INNOCENT	BYRON	PROMETHEUS	LETTERS	GUILTY
ENGLAND	MORITZ	CONFUSION	KIRWIN	FRIENDSHIP

Frankenstein

SCOTLAND	MARY	GUILTY	PROMETHEUS	SCARLET
ALPHONSE	WALDMAN	CHEMISTRY	LACEY	FOOD
MORITZ	BYRON	FREE SPACE	CORNELIUS	SAFIE
ENGLAND	VICTOR	FRIENDSHIP	LIGHT	CAROLINE
READ	DISGUST	LOCKET	FEMALE	WILLIAM

Frankenstein

INNOCENT	KIRWIN	LETTERS	ARCTIC	ERNEST
GENEVA	WALTON	KREMPE	HENRY	LIFE
REMORSE	CREATURE	FREE SPACE	CONFUSION	ALPS
PERCY	FELIX	INGOLSTADT	ELIZABETH	FRANKENSTEIN
WILLIAM	FEMALE	LOCKET	DISGUST	READ

Frankenstein

GENEVA	FRIENDSHIP	LETTERS	LIFE	INNOCENT
MORITZ	ERNEST	VICTOR	CONFUSION	CORNELIUS
CREATURE	ELIZABETH	FREE SPACE	CHEMISTRY	SCOTLAND
PROMETHEUS	ENGLAND	KREMPE	REMORSE	LACEY
DISGUST	MARY	OBSERVATION	SCARLET	WILLIAM

Frankenstein

LOCKET	GUILTY	FOOD	SAFIE	FEMALE
FRANKENSTEIN	READ	ALPHONSE	HENRY	LIGHT
INGOLSTADT	WALTON	FREE SPACE	ARCTIC	THREE
PERCY	CAROLINE	BYRON	KIRWIN	WALDMAN
WILLIAM	SCARLET	OBSERVATION	MARY	DISGUST

Frankenstein

CONFUSION	INGOLSTADT	DISGUST	FRIENDSHIP	SAFIE
WALDMAN	LIGHT	THREE	INNOCENT	ELIZABETH
PERCY	CAROLINE	FREE SPACE	CREATURE	KREMPE
READ	SCOTLAND	LACEY	GUILTY	CORNELIUS
WILLIAM	ARCTIC	CHEMISTRY	MARY	WALTON

Frankenstein

FRANKENSTEIN	LIFE	LOCKET	GENEVA	ENGLAND
BYRON	FEMALE	SCARLET	HENRY	FELIX
REMORSE	MORITZ	FREE SPACE	ERNEST	VICTOR
PROMETHEUS	LETTERS	KIRWIN	OBSERVATION	FOOD
WALTON	MARY	CHEMISTRY	ARCTIC	WILLIAM

Frankenstein

LOCKET	VICTOR	WALDMAN	LIGHT	PROMETHEUS
MORITZ	PERCY	GENEVA	WILLIAM	LIFE
HENRY	LACEY	FREE SPACE	FRANKENSTEIN	BYRON
DISGUST	ERNEST	WALTON	SCARLET	CHEMISTRY
ENGLAND	ELIZABETH	CREATURE	CAROLINE	FELIX

Frankenstein

THREE	INGOLSTADT	FOOD	FRIENDSHIP	ALPHONSE
GUILTY	KIRWIN	REMORSE	CORNELIUS	KREMPE
LETTERS	FEMALE	FREE SPACE	SAFIE	ARCTIC
OBSERVATION	CONFUSION	SCOTLAND	MARY	READ
FELIX	CAROLINE	CREATURE	ELIZABETH	ENGLAND

Frankenstein

CONFUSION	FEMALE	WALDMAN	LACEY	ENGLAND
FRIENDSHIP	THREE	BYRON	ELIZABETH	LOCKET
GENEVA	SCOTLAND	FREE SPACE	KREMPE	VICTOR
FELIX	READ	LIFE	CORNELIUS	SCARLET
LETTERS	SAFIE	WALTON	OBSERVATION	REMORSE

Frankenstein

WILLIAM	ALPS	GUILTY	INGOLSTADT	PROMETHEUS
HENRY	FOOD	PERCY	MARY	DISGUST
CAROLINE	ALPHONSE	FREE SPACE	ARCTIC	CHEMISTRY
CREATURE	ERNEST	MORITZ	INNOCENT	FRANKENSTEIN
REMORSE	OBSERVATION	WALTON	SAFIE	LETTERS

Frankenstein

KREMPE	OBSERVATION	INGOLSTADT	CORNELIUS	PERCY
READ	MORITZ	DISGUST	CONFUSION	ALPHONSE
FOOD	KIRWIN	FREE SPACE	GUILTY	ELIZABETH
BYRON	HENRY	LIFE	VICTOR	SCARLET
FEMALE	REMORSE	LETTERS	FRIENDSHIP	FRANKENSTEIN

Frankenstein

CAROLINE	MARY	ALPS	ENGLAND	WALTON
ERNEST	WALDMAN	PROMETHEUS	CREATURE	WILLIAM
THREE	LIGHT	FREE SPACE	LOCKET	SAFIE
CHEMISTRY	ARCTIC	LACEY	GENEVA	FELIX
FRANKENSTEIN	FRIENDSHIP	LETTERS	REMORSE	FEMALE

Frankenstein

CONFUSION	FRANKENSTEIN	LIGHT	PROMETHEUS	ENGLAND
GUILTY	INNOCENT	SCARLET	ELIZABETH	KREMPE
MARY	WALTON	FREE SPACE	CREATURE	ERNEST
LACEY	WILLIAM	SCOTLAND	ALPS	DISGUST
VICTOR	FOOD	REMORSE	INGOLSTADT	ARCTIC

Frankenstein

READ	THREE	WALDMAN	HENRY	PERCY
OBSERVATION	BYRON	LETTERS	SAFIE	ALPHONSE
LOCKET	FRIENDSHIP	FREE SPACE	CORNELIUS	CHEMISTRY
FELIX	GENEVA	MORITZ	CAROLINE	FEMALE
ARCTIC	INGOLSTADT	REMORSE	FOOD	VICTOR

Frankenstein

KIRWIN	LIGHT	VICTOR	ERNEST	CHEMISTRY
GENEVA	FELIX	INNOCENT	CORNELIUS	WILLIAM
OBSERVATION	REMORSE	FREE SPACE	DISGUST	WALTON
GUILTY	MARY	BYRON	CONFUSION	PROMETHEUS
INGOLSTADT	ENGLAND	CREATURE	ARCTIC	SCOTLAND

Frankenstein

WALDMAN	PERCY	THREE	READ	ELIZABETH
CAROLINE	FEMALE	ALPS	LACEY	FRANKENSTEIN
LOCKET	MORITZ	FREE SPACE	LETTERS	SCARLET
SAFIE	KREMPE	FRIENDSHIP	LIFE	HENRY
SCOTLAND	ARCTIC	CREATURE	ENGLAND	INGOLSTADT

Frankenstein

PROMETHEUS	DISGUST	FEMALE	ALPS	CHEMISTRY
VICTOR	READ	CONFUSION	GENEVA	MORITZ
ERNEST	SCOTLAND	FREE SPACE	ENGLAND	REMORSE
FELIX	LIFE	SAFIE	ELIZABETH	ARCTIC
INGOLSTADT	FRIENDSHIP	INNOCENT	HENRY	LOCKET

Frankenstein

LIGHT	THREE	ALPHONSE	CAROLINE	MARY
LETTERS	BYRON	CORNELIUS	GUILTY	OBSERVATION
WALDMAN	FRANKENSTEIN	FREE SPACE	PERCY	KREMPE
KIRWIN	CREATURE	WILLIAM	WALTON	LACEY
LOCKET	HENRY	INNOCENT	FRIENDSHIP	INGOLSTADT

Frankenstein

SCOTLAND	CONFUSION	REMORSE	CORNELIUS	FRIENDSHIP
WALDMAN	ARCTIC	SCARLET	KIRWIN	ERNEST
WALTON	VICTOR	FREE SPACE	HENRY	INNOCENT
BYRON	GUILTY	LACEY	CAROLINE	LIGHT
KREMPE	LETTERS	ENGLAND	PERCY	MARY

Frankenstein

FELIX	GENEVA	INGOLSTADT	LIFE	ALPHONSE
LOCKET	DISGUST	PROMETHEUS	THREE	CREATURE
CHEMISTRY	SAFIE	FREE SPACE	FEMALE	MORITZ
WILLIAM	FRANKENSTEIN	OBSERVATION	ALPS	FOOD
MARY	PERCY	ENGLAND	LETTERS	KREMPE

Frankenstein

FOOD	OBSERVATION	INGOLSTADT	ERNEST	KIRWIN
LIFE	REMORSE	ALPHONSE	FEMALE	ENGLAND
LACEY	GENEVA	FREE SPACE	ALPS	LOCKET
DISGUST	PROMETHEUS	READ	FRANKENSTEIN	CAROLINE
PERCY	MORITZ	CORNELIUS	WALTON	LETTERS

Frankenstein

MARY	SCOTLAND	INNOCENT	CREATURE	HENRY
SCARLET	VICTOR	ARCTIC	GUILTY	FRIENDSHIP
CHEMISTRY	KREMPE	FREE SPACE	BYRON	CONFUSION
THREE	WILLIAM	FELIX	LIGHT	WALDMAN
LETTERS	WALTON	CORNELIUS	MORITZ	PERCY

Frankenstein Vocabulary Word List

No.	Word	Clue/Definition
1.	ABHORRENT	Hateful; detestable
2.	APPALLING	Shocking
3.	ARDENT	Passionate; enthusiastic
4.	AUGMENTED	Increased; added to
5.	BENEVOLENT	Generous
6.	CALAMITY	Disaster
7.	CAPACIOUS	Spacious; roomy
8.	CAPRICE	Whim
9.	CARNAGE	Destruction or wreckage of life
10.	COMMISERATE	Feel sympathy for
11.	CONFLAGRATION	A great fire
12.	COUNTENANCE	Facial features
13.	CURSORY	Hastily done
14.	DEBILITATED	Weakened; made unable
15.	DETRIMENTAL	Harmful; damaging
16.	DIABOLICAL	Devilish
17.	DILATE	Expand
18.	EMACIATED	Thin and wasted
19.	EPITHETS	Abusive words
20.	EXHORTATIONS	Urgings
21.	EXPEDIENT	Suitable; practical
22.	FETTER	Shackle
23.	HARROWING	Distressing; agonizing
24.	IGNOMINIOUS	Disgraceful
25.	IMMUTABLE	Unchanging
26.	IMPERIOUS	Domineering
27.	INCLEMENCY	Storminess
28.	INDEFATIGABLE	Tireless
29.	INDOLENCE	Laziness
30.	INEXORABLE	Relentless; unyielding
31.	INTERMENT	Burial
32.	LANGUID	Lacking energy
33.	OBDURATE	Stubborn
34.	OBLITERATED	Destroyed completely
35.	OBLIVION	Forgotten; forgetfulness
36.	ODIOUS	Hateful
37.	PAROXYSM	Spasm; convulsion
38.	PENURY	Extreme poverty
39.	PERDITION	Complete ruin
40.	PHYSIOGNOMY	Face
41.	PORTEND	Predict
42.	POSTERITY	Future generations
43.	PRECIPITOUS	Steep
44.	PROGENY	Children; offspring
45.	PROGNOSTICATED	Predicted
46.	PURLOINED	Stolen
47.	RANKLING	Irritating
48.	REPUGNANCE	Loathing; repulsiveness
49.	RETROSPECT	Looking back on the past
50.	REVERIES	Daydreams
51.	SALUBRIOUS	Healthful

Frankenstein Vocabulary Word List Continued

No.	Word	Clue/Definition
52.	SANGUINARY	Accompanied by carnage; bloodthirsty
53.	SATIATED	Fully satisfied
54.	SLAKED	Quenched
55.	SOPHISMS	Misleading arguments
56.	SUSTENANCE	Means of nourishment
57.	TIMOROUS	Fearful
58.	VACILLATING	Fluctuating; wavering
59.	WANTONLY	Immorally; cruelly
60.	WRETCHED	Miserable

Frankenstein Vocabulary Fill In The Blank 1

_____ 1. Fearful

_____ 2. Facial features

_____ 3. Hastily done

_____ 4. Harmful; damaging

_____ 5. Means of nourishment

_____ 6. Unchanging

_____ 7. Spacious; roomy

_____ 8. Children; offspring

_____ 9. Forgotten; forgetfulness

_____ 10. Accompanied by carnage; bloodthirsty

_____ 11. Generous

_____ 12. Abusive words

_____ 13. Disaster

_____ 14. Complete ruin

_____ 15. Thin and wasted

_____ 16. Lacking energy

_____ 17. Stubborn

_____ 18. Expand

_____ 19. Future generations

_____ 20. Daydreams

Frankenstein Vocabulary Fill In The Blank 1 Answer Key

TIMOROUS	1. Fearful
COUNTENANCE	2. Facial features
CURSORY	3. Hastily done
DETRIMENTAL	4. Harmful; damaging
SUSTENANCE	5. Means of nourishment
IMMUTABLE	6. Unchanging
CAPACIOUS	7. Spacious; roomy
PROGENY	8. Children; offspring
OBLIVION	9. Forgotten; forgetfulness
SANGUINARY	10. Accompanied by carnage; bloodthirsty
BENEVOLENT	11. Generous
EPITHETS	12. Abusive words
CALAMITY	13. Disaster
PERDITION	14. Complete ruin
EMACIATED	15. Thin and wasted
LANGUID	16. Lacking energy
OBDURATE	17. Stubborn
DILATE	18. Expand
POSTERITY	19. Future generations
REVERIES	20. Daydreams

Frankenstein Vocabulary Fill In The Blank 2

_____   1. Looking back on the past
_____   2. Laziness
_____   3. Hateful; detestable
_____   4. Relentless; unyielding
_____   5. Miserable
_____   6. Disaster
_____   7. Feel sympathy for
_____   8. Tireless
_____   9. Quenched
_____ 10. Immorally; cruelly
_____ 11. Fluctuating; wavering
_____ 12. Misleading arguments
_____ 13. Future generations
_____ 14. Loathing; repulsiveness
_____ 15. Destruction or wreckage of life
_____ 16. Generous
_____ 17. Whim
_____ 18. Harmful; damaging
_____ 19. Hastily done
_____ 20. Irritating

Frankenstein Vocabulary Fill In The Blank 2 Answer Key

RETROSPECT	1. Looking back on the past
INDOLENCE	2. Laziness
ABHORRENT	3. Hateful; detestable
INEXORABLE	4. Relentless; unyielding
WRETCHED	5. Miserable
CALAMITY	6. Disaster
COMMISERATE	7. Feel sympathy for
INDEFATIGABLE	8. Tireless
SLAKED	9. Quenched
WANTONLY	10. Immorally; cruelly
VACILLATING	11. Fluctuating; wavering
SOPHISMS	12. Misleading arguments
POSTERITY	13. Future generations
REPUGNANCE	14. Loathing; repulsiveness
CARNAGE	15. Destruction or wreckage of life
BENEVOLENT	16. Generous
CAPRICE	17. Whim
DETRIMENTAL	18. Harmful; damaging
CURSORY	19. Hastily done
RANKLING	20. Irritating

Frankenstein Vocabulary Fill In The Blank 3

_____ 1. Forgotten; forgetfulness
_____ 2. Irritating
_____ 3. Burial
_____ 4. Destruction or wreckage of life
_____ 5. Passionate; enthusiastic
_____ 6. Predict
_____ 7. Extreme poverty
_____ 8. Disgraceful
_____ 9. Predicted
_____ 10. Face
_____ 11. Tireless
_____ 12. Lacking energy
_____ 13. Healthful
_____ 14. Facial features
_____ 15. Devilish
_____ 16. Laziness
_____ 17. Expand
_____ 18. Storminess
_____ 19. Disaster
_____ 20. Destroyed completely

Frankenstein Vocabulary Fill In The Blank 3 Answer Key

OBLIVION	1. Forgotten; forgetfulness
RANKLING	2. Irritating
INTERMENT	3. Burial
CARNAGE	4. Destruction or wreckage of life
ARDENT	5. Passionate; enthusiastic
PORTEND	6. Predict
PENURY	7. Extreme poverty
IGNOMINIOUS	8. Disgraceful
PROGNOSTICATED	9. Predicted
PHYSIOGNOMY	10. Face
INDEFATIGABLE	11. Tireless
LANGUID	12. Lacking energy
SALUBRIOUS	13. Healthful
COUNTENANCE	14. Facial features
DIABOLICAL	15. Devilish
INDOLENCE	16. Laziness
DILATE	17. Expand
INCLEMENCY	18. Storminess
CALAMITY	19. Disaster
OBLITERATED	20. Destroyed completely

Frankenstein Vocabulary Fill In The Blank 4

_____ 1. Increased; added to
_____ 2. Accompanied by carnage; bloodthirsty
_____ 3. Stolen
_____ 4. Means of nourishment
_____ 5. Harmful; damaging
_____ 6. Extreme poverty
_____ 7. Unchanging
_____ 8. Whim
_____ 9. Miserable
_____ 10. Misleading arguments
_____ 11. Domineering
_____ 12. A great fire
_____ 13. Healthful
_____ 14. Destruction or wreckage of life
_____ 15. Hateful; detestable
_____ 16. Quenched
_____ 17. Predict
_____ 18. Spasm; convulsion
_____ 19. Expand
_____ 20. Relentless; unyielding

Frankenstein Vocabulary Fill In The Blank 4 Answer Key

AUGMENTED	1. Increased; added to
SANGUINARY	2. Accompanied by carnage; bloodthirsty
PURLOINED	3. Stolen
SUSTENANCE	4. Means of nourishment
DETRIMENTAL	5. Harmful; damaging
PENURY	6. Extreme poverty
IMMUTABLE	7. Unchanging
CAPRICE	8. Whim
WRETCHED	9. Miserable
SOPHISMS	10. Misleading arguments
IMPERIOUS	11. Domineering
CONFLAGRATION	12. A great fire
SALUBRIOUS	13. Healthful
CARNAGE	14. Destruction or wreckage of life
ABHORRENT	15. Hateful; detestable
SLAKED	16. Quenched
PORTEND	17. Predict
PAROXYSM	18. Spasm; convulsion
DILATE	19. Expand
INEXORABLE	20. Relentless; unyielding

Frankenstein Vocabulary Matching 1

___ 1. ARDENT   A. Loathing; repulsiveness
___ 2. SANGUINARY B. Increased; added to
___ 3. INTERMENT   C. Unchanging
___ 4. IMMUTABLE   D. Passionate; enthusiastic
___ 5. RETROSPECT E. Shackle
___ 6. DILATE   F. Fluctuating; wavering
___ 7. HARROWING   G. Looking back on the past
___ 8. REPUGNANCE H. Facial features
___ 9. INEXORABLE I. Hateful; detestable
___10. SLAKED   J. Healthful
___11. EMACIATED   K. Relentless; unyielding
___12. FETTER   L. Feel sympathy for
___13. COUNTENANCE M. Predict
___14. AUGMENTED   N. Burial
___15. REVERIES   O. Disgraceful
___16. PROGENY   P. Accompanied by carnage; bloodthirsty
___17. VACILLATING Q. Shocking
___18. PORTEND   R. Thin and wasted
___19. SALUBRIOUS S. Quenched
___20. COMMISERATE T. Abusive words
___21. APPALLING   U. Expand
___22. EPITHETS   V. Laziness
___23. ABHORRENT   W. Daydreams
___24. IGNOMINIOUS X. Distressing; agonizing
___25. INDOLENCE   Y. Children; offspring

Frankenstein Vocabulary Matching 1 Answer Key

D - 1. ARDENT	A.	Loathing; repulsiveness
P - 2. SANGUINARY	B.	Increased; added to
N - 3. INTERMENT	C.	Unchanging
C - 4. IMMUTABLE	D.	Passionate; enthusiastic
G - 5. RETROSPECT	E.	Shackle
U - 6. DILATE	F.	Fluctuating; wavering
X - 7. HARROWING	G.	Looking back on the past
A - 8. REPUGNANCE	H.	Facial features
K - 9. INEXORABLE	I.	Hateful; detestable
S - 10. SLAKED	J.	Healthful
R - 11. EMACIATED	K.	Relentless; unyielding
E - 12. FETTER	L.	Feel sympathy for
H - 13. COUNTENANCE	M.	Predict
B - 14. AUGMENTED	N.	Burial
W - 15. REVERIES	O.	Disgraceful
Y - 16. PROGENY	P.	Accompanied by carnage; bloodthirsty
F - 17. VACILLATING	Q.	Shocking
M - 18. PORTEND	R.	Thin and wasted
J - 19. SALUBRIOUS	S.	Quenched
L - 20. COMMISERATE	T.	Abusive words
Q - 21. APPALLING	U.	Expand
T - 22. EPITHETS	V.	Laziness
I - 23. ABHORRENT	W.	Daydreams
O - 24. IGNOMINIOUS	X.	Distressing; agonizing
V - 25. INDOLENCE	Y.	Children; offspring

Frankenstein Vocabulary Matching 2

___ 1. DEBILITATED A. Destroyed completely
___ 2. VACILLATING B. Weakened; made unable
___ 3. EPITHETS C. Miserable
___ 4. INDEFATIGABLE D. Distressing; agonizing
___ 5. RETROSPECT E. Extreme poverty
___ 6. LANGUID F. Fluctuating; wavering
___ 7. SANGUINARY G. Immorally; cruelly
___ 8. CURSORY H. Misleading arguments
___ 9. REPUGNANCE I. Shocking
___10. SOPHISMS J. A great fire
___11. PENURY K. Daydreams
___12. AUGMENTED L. Children; offspring
___13. REVERIES M. Looking back on the past
___14. SALUBRIOUS N. Tireless
___15. WRETCHED O. Lacking energy
___16. WANTONLY P. Accompanied by carnage; bloodthirsty
___17. INDOLENCE Q. Urgings
___18. COMMISERATE R. Loathing; repulsiveness
___19. PROGENY S. Laziness
___20. EXHORTATIONS T. Feel sympathy for
___21. APPALLING U. Predicted
___22. OBLITERATED V. Healthful
___23. CONFLAGRATION W. Increased; added to
___24. HARROWING X. Hastily done
___25. PROGNOSTICATED Y. Abusive words

Frankenstein Vocabulary Matching 2 Answer Key

B - 1.	DEBILITATED	A. Destroyed completely
F - 2.	VACILLATING	B. Weakened; made unable
Y - 3.	EPITHETS	C. Miserable
N - 4.	INDEFATIGABLE	D. Distressing; agonizing
M - 5.	RETROSPECT	E. Extreme poverty
O - 6.	LANGUID	F. Fluctuating; wavering
P - 7.	SANGUINARY	G. Immorally; cruelly
X - 8.	CURSORY	H. Misleading arguments
R - 9.	REPUGNANCE	I. Shocking
H - 10.	SOPHISMS	J. A great fire
E - 11.	PENURY	K. Daydreams
W - 12.	AUGMENTED	L. Children; offspring
K - 13.	REVERIES	M. Looking back on the past
V - 14.	SALUBRIOUS	N. Tireless
C - 15.	WRETCHED	O. Lacking energy
G - 16.	WANTONLY	P. Accompanied by carnage; bloodthirsty
S - 17.	INDOLENCE	Q. Urgings
T - 18.	COMMISERATE	R. Loathing; repulsiveness
L - 19.	PROGENY	S. Laziness
Q - 20.	EXHORTATIONS	T. Feel sympathy for
I - 21.	APPALLING	U. Predicted
A - 22.	OBLITERATED	V. Healthful
J - 23.	CONFLAGRATION	W. Increased; added to
D - 24.	HARROWING	X. Hastily done
U - 25.	PROGNOSTICATED	Y. Abusive words

Frankenstein Vocabulary Matching 3

___ 1. BENEVOLENT   A. Suitable; practical
___ 2. LANGUID   B. Forgotten; forgetfulness
___ 3. CURSORY   C. Quenched
___ 4. EXHORTATIONS   D. Lacking energy
___ 5. DILATE   E. Fearful
___ 6. FETTER   F. Means of nourishment
___ 7. PORTEND   G. Urgings
___ 8. SLAKED   H. Irritating
___ 9. EXPEDIENT   I. Predict
___10. SUSTENANCE   J. Loathing; repulsiveness
___11. DIABOLICAL   K. Shackle
___12. INDOLENCE   L. Passionate; enthusiastic
___13. REPUGNANCE   M. Misleading arguments
___14. ARDENT   N. Disaster
___15. RANKLING   O. Devilish
___16. CALAMITY   P. Burial
___17. ODIOUS   Q. Laziness
___18. SOPHISMS   R. Generous
___19. IMPERIOUS   S. Hastily done
___20. RETROSPECT   T. Children; offspring
___21. OBLIVION   U. Looking back on the past
___22. INTERMENT   V. Hateful
___23. TIMOROUS   W. Expand
___24. PAROXYSM   X. Domineering
___25. PROGENY   Y. Spasm; convulsion

Frankenstein Vocabulary Matching 3 Answer Key

R - 1. BENEVOLENT		A. Suitable; practical
D - 2. LANGUID		B. Forgotten; forgetfulness
S - 3. CURSORY		C. Quenched
G - 4. EXHORTATIONS		D. Lacking energy
W - 5. DILATE		E. Fearful
K - 6. FETTER		F. Means of nourishment
I - 7. PORTEND		G. Urgings
C - 8. SLAKED		H. Irritating
A - 9. EXPEDIENT		I. Predict
F - 10. SUSTENANCE		J. Loathing; repulsiveness
O - 11. DIABOLICAL		K. Shackle
Q - 12. INDOLENCE		L. Passionate; enthusiastic
J - 13. REPUGNANCE		M. Misleading arguments
L - 14. ARDENT		N. Disaster
H - 15. RANKLING		O. Devilish
N - 16. CALAMITY		P. Burial
V - 17. ODIOUS		Q. Laziness
M - 18. SOPHISMS		R. Generous
X - 19. IMPERIOUS		S. Hastily done
U - 20. RETROSPECT		T. Children; offspring
B - 21. OBLIVION		U. Looking back on the past
P - 22. INTERMENT		V. Hateful
E - 23. TIMOROUS		W. Expand
Y - 24. PAROXYSM		X. Domineering
T - 25. PROGENY		Y. Spasm; convulsion

Frankenstein Vocabulary Matching 4

___ 1. REVERIES	A. Feel sympathy for
___ 2. LANGUID	B. Generous
___ 3. PAROXYSM	C. Lacking energy
___ 4. EXHORTATIONS	D. Harmful; damaging
___ 5. CARNAGE	E. Urgings
___ 6. PORTEND	F. Means of nourishment
___ 7. OBDURATE	G. Unchanging
___ 8. HARROWING	H. Hastily done
___ 9. SLAKED	I. Quenched
___10. DEBILITATED	J. Children; offspring
___11. TIMOROUS	K. Weakened; made unable
___12. APPALLING	L. Domineering
___13. SUSTENANCE	M. Fearful
___14. EXPEDIENT	N. Distressing; agonizing
___15. IMPERIOUS	O. Shocking
___16. DETRIMENTAL	P. Relentless; unyielding
___17. CURSORY	Q. Destruction or wreckage of life
___18. IMMUTABLE	R. Daydreams
___19. VACILLATING	S. Predict
___20. CAPACIOUS	T. Stubborn
___21. PHYSIOGNOMY	U. Suitable; practical
___22. COMMISERATE	V. Spacious; roomy
___23. PROGENY	W. Spasm; convulsion
___24. BENEVOLENT	X. Face
___25. INEXORABLE	Y. Fluctuating; wavering

Frankenstein Vocabulary Matching 4 Answer Key

R - 1.	REVERIES	A.	Feel sympathy for
C - 2.	LANGUID	B.	Generous
W - 3.	PAROXYSM	C.	Lacking energy
E - 4.	EXHORTATIONS	D.	Harmful; damaging
Q - 5.	CARNAGE	E.	Urgings
S - 6.	PORTEND	F.	Means of nourishment
T - 7.	OBDURATE	G.	Unchanging
N - 8.	HARROWING	H.	Hastily done
I - 9.	SLAKED	I.	Quenched
K - 10.	DEBILITATED	J.	Children; offspring
M - 11.	TIMOROUS	K.	Weakened; made unable
O - 12.	APPALLING	L.	Domineering
F - 13.	SUSTENANCE	M.	Fearful
U - 14.	EXPEDIENT	N.	Distressing; agonizing
L - 15.	IMPERIOUS	O.	Shocking
D - 16.	DETRIMENTAL	P.	Relentless; unyielding
H - 17.	CURSORY	Q.	Destruction or wreckage of life
G - 18.	IMMUTABLE	R.	Daydreams
Y - 19.	VACILLATING	S.	Predict
V - 20.	CAPACIOUS	T.	Stubborn
X - 21.	PHYSIOGNOMY	U.	Suitable; practical
A - 22.	COMMISERATE	V.	Spacious; roomy
J - 23.	PROGENY	W.	Spasm; convulsion
B - 24.	BENEVOLENT	X.	Face
P - 25.	INEXORABLE	Y.	Fluctuating; wavering

Frankenstein Vocabulary Magic Squares 1

Match the definition with the vocabulary word. Put your answers in the magic squares below. When your answers are correct, all columns and rows will add to the same number.

A. SATIATED
B. EMACIATED
C. EXHORTATIONS
D. COUNTENANCE
E. INCLEMENCY
F. PAROXYSM
G. INTERMENT
H. INDOLENCE
I. DIABOLICAL
J. REPUGNANCE
K. SANGUINARY
L. RANKLING
M. AUGMENTED
N. DEBILITATED
O. ABHORRENT
P. APPALLING

1. Hateful; detestable
2. Loathing; repulsiveness
3. Laziness
4. Fully satisfied
5. Facial features
6. Storminess
7. Accompanied by carnage; bloodthirsty
8. Weakened; made unable
9. Spasm; convulsion
10. Urgings
11. Increased; added to
12. Irritating
13. Devilish
14. Shocking
15. Thin and wasted
16. Burial

A=	B=	C=	D=
E=	F=	G=	H=
I=	J=	K=	L=
M=	N=	O=	P=

Frankenstein Vocabulary Magic Squares 1 Answer Key

Match the definition with the vocabulary word. Put your answers in the magic squares below. When your answers are correct, all columns and rows will add to the same number.

A. SATIATED
B. EMACIATED
C. EXHORTATIONS
D. COUNTENANCE
E. INCLEMENCY
F. PAROXYSM
G. INTERMENT
H. INDOLENCE
I. DIABOLICAL
J. REPUGNANCE
K. SANGUINARY
L. RANKLING
M. AUGMENTED
N. DEBILITATED
O. ABHORRENT
P. APPALLING

1. Hateful; detestable
2. Loathing; repulsiveness
3. Laziness
4. Fully satisfied
5. Facial features
6. Storminess
7. Accompanied by carnage; bloodthirsty
8. Weakened; made unable
9. Spasm; convulsion
10. Urgings
11. Increased; added to
12. Irritating
13. Devilish
14. Shocking
15. Thin and wasted
16. Burial

A=4	B=15	C=10	D=5
E=6	F=9	G=16	H=3
I=13	J=2	K=7	L=12
M=11	N=8	O=1	P=14

Frankenstein Vocabulary Magic Squares 2

Match the definition with the vocabulary word. Put your answers in the magic squares below. When your answers are correct, all columns and rows will add to the same number.

A. ABHORRENT
B. SOPHISMS
C. SALUBRIOUS
D. FETTER
E. CALAMITY
F. CAPACIOUS
G. CURSORY
H. DILATE
I. DEBILITATED
J. BENEVOLENT
K. IGNOMINIOUS
L. PHYSIOGNOMY
M. IMMUTABLE
N. ARDENT
O. IMPERIOUS
P. SUSTENANCE

1. Domineering
2. Shackle
3. Generous
4. Disaster
5. Weakened; made unable
6. Spacious; roomy
7. Means of nourishment
8. Healthful
9. Expand
10. Disgraceful
11. Hateful; detestable
12. Passionate; enthusiastic
13. Misleading arguments
14. Unchanging
15. Hastily done
16. Face

A=	B=	C=	D=
E=	F=	G=	H=
I=	J=	K=	L=
M=	N=	O=	P=

Frankenstein Vocabulary Magic Squares 2 Answer Key

Match the definition with the vocabulary word. Put your answers in the magic squares below. When your answers are correct, all columns and rows will add to the same number.

A. ABHORRENT
B. SOPHISMS
C. SALUBRIOUS
D. FETTER
E. CALAMITY
F. CAPACIOUS
G. CURSORY
H. DILATE
I. DEBILITATED
J. BENEVOLENT
K. IGNOMINIOUS
L. PHYSIOGNOMY
M. IMMUTABLE
N. ARDENT
O. IMPERIOUS
P. SUSTENANCE

1. Domineering
2. Shackle
3. Generous
4. Disaster
5. Weakened; made unable
6. Spacious; roomy
7. Means of nourishment
8. Healthful
9. Expand
10. Disgraceful
11. Hateful; detestable
12. Passionate; enthusiastic
13. Misleading arguments
14. Unchanging
15. Hastily done
16. Face

A=11	B=13	C=8	D=2
E=4	F=6	G=15	H=9
I=5	J=3	K=10	L=16
M=14	N=12	O=1	P=7

Frankenstein Vocabulary Magic Squares 3

Match the definition with the vocabulary word. Put your answers in the magic squares below. When your answers are correct, all columns and rows will add to the same number.

A. INTERMENT
B. ARDENT
C. IGNOMINIOUS
D. DIABOLICAL
E. HARROWING
F. COUNTENANCE
G. PROGNOSTICATED
H. OBLIVION
I. CAPRICE
J. INDOLENCE
K. PENURY
L. REPUGNANCE
M. CALAMITY
N. EXPEDIENT
O. OBDURATE
P. COMMISERATE

1. Disgraceful
2. Laziness
3. Facial features
4. Stubborn
5. Feel sympathy for
6. Distressing; agonizing
7. Whim
8. Devilish
9. Disaster
10. Forgotten; forgetfulness
11. Loathing; repulsiveness
12. Burial
13. Passionate; enthusiastic
14. Extreme poverty
15. Predicted
16. Suitable; practical

A=	B=	C=	D=
E=	F=	G=	H=
I=	J=	K=	L=
M=	N=	O=	P=

Frankenstein Vocabulary Magic Squares 3 Answer Key

Match the definition with the vocabulary word. Put your answers in the magic squares below. When your answers are correct, all columns and rows will add to the same number.

A. INTERMENT
B. ARDENT
C. IGNOMINIOUS
D. DIABOLICAL
E. HARROWING
F. COUNTENANCE
G. PROGNOSTICATED
H. OBLIVION
I. CAPRICE
J. INDOLENCE
K. PENURY
L. REPUGNANCE
M. CALAMITY
N. EXPEDIENT
O. OBDURATE
P. COMMISERATE

1. Disgraceful
2. Laziness
3. Facial features
4. Stubborn
5. Feel sympathy for
6. Distressing; agonizing
7. Whim
8. Devilish
9. Disaster
10. Forgotten; forgetfulness
11. Loathing; repulsiveness
12. Burial
13. Passionate; enthusiastic
14. Extreme poverty
15. Predicted
16. Suitable; practical

A=12	B=13	C=1	D=8
E=6	F=3	G=15	H=10
I=7	J=2	K=14	L=11
M=9	N=16	O=4	P=5

Frankenstein Vocabulary Magic Squares 4

Match the definition with the vocabulary word. Put your answers in the magic squares below. When your answers are correct, all columns and rows will add to the same number.

A. CAPRICE
B. PHYSIOGNOMY
C. PENURY
D. LANGUID
E. OBLIVION
F. EPITHETS
G. PURLOINED
H. RANKLING
I. SOPHISMS
J. PORTEND
K. CAPACIOUS
L. PROGENY
M. INEXORABLE
N. POSTERITY
O. SALUBRIOUS
P. SLAKED

1. Abusive words
2. Misleading arguments
3. Healthful
4. Lacking energy
5. Relentless; unyielding
6. Face
7. Irritating
8. Spacious; roomy
9. Extreme poverty
10. Quenched
11. Predict
12. Forgotten; forgetfulness
13. Children; offspring
14. Stolen
15. Whim
16. Future generations

A=	B=	C=	D=
E=	F=	G=	H=
I=	J=	K=	L=
M=	N=	O=	P=

Frankenstein Vocabulary Magic Squares 4 Answer Key

Match the definition with the vocabulary word. Put your answers in the magic squares below. When your answers are correct, all columns and rows will add to the same number.

A. CAPRICE
B. PHYSIOGNOMY
C. PENURY
D. LANGUID
E. OBLIVION
F. EPITHETS
G. PURLOINED
H. RANKLING
I. SOPHISMS
J. PORTEND
K. CAPACIOUS
L. PROGENY
M. INEXORABLE
N. POSTERITY
O. SALUBRIOUS
P. SLAKED

1. Abusive words
2. Misleading arguments
3. Healthful
4. Lacking energy
5. Relentless; unyielding
6. Face
7. Irritating
8. Spacious; roomy
9. Extreme poverty
10. Quenched
11. Predict
12. Forgotten; forgetfulness
13. Children; offspring
14. Stolen
15. Whim
16. Future generations

A=15	B=6	C=9	D=4
E=12	F=1	G=14	H=7
I=2	J=11	K=8	L=13
M=5	N=16	O=3	P=10

Frankenstein Vocabulary Word Search 1

```
H A R R O W I N G Y I D S I V F E C W L
P U P K W P T F R G D E K M J N X O Y V
Z G E W X L Q U N Y G H M M W P P N E K
S M R R B C N O R W J C Y U K M E F X Z
O E D D N E M Z M Y Z T S T Q Y D L H F
P N I E P I T H E T S E O A J T I A O V
H T T C N Y I N E X O R A B L E E G R Q
I E I I A R D N P Z Z W R L L T N R T Y
S D O L J P P E S O V S H E A I T A A N
M U N D M Q A Q T J S N B L W R V T T Y
S U O T I P I C E R P T I X A C D I I K
S A L W N O A U I F I D E N X N M O O N
R A N W V P U R C O G M K R Q C G N N N
S E T G R K X S C M U L E Q I P W U S H
U T T I U D D O H A I S Z N R T V A I J
S N C R A I C R I N R Z L O T A Y P N D
T E O T O T N Y G N L N G A C A D P T T
E R B Y I S E A R C D E A I K E L A E W
N R D L D M P D R E N O L G N E D L R W F
A O U N P R O E S Y V L L I E N D L M R
N H R O E C Z R C S A E O E E F N I E D
C B A T P M S L O T G L R T N L R N N W
E A T N E D R A I U R Z R I S C J G T G
X E E A Z M H N X U S O V P E C E Y V C
F S Q W Y X G K P C P X C F G S J D D W
```

A great fire (13)
Abusive words (8)
Accompanied by carnage; bloodthirsty (10)
Burial (9)
Children; offspring (7)
Complete ruin (9)
Daydreams (8)
Destruction or wreckage of life (7)
Disgraceful (11)
Distressing; agonizing (9)
Expand (6)
Extreme poverty (6)
Fearful (8)
Fluctuating; wavering (11)
Forgotten; forgetfulness (8)
Fully satisfied (8)
Future generations (9)
Harmful; damaging (11)
Hastily done (7)
Hateful (6)
Hateful; detestable (9)
Immorally; cruelly (8)
Increased; added to (9)

Irritating (8)
Lacking energy (7)
Laziness (9)
Looking back on the past (10)
Means of nourishment (10)
Miserable (8)
Misleading arguments (8)
Passionate; enthusiastic (6)
Predict (7)
Quenched (6)
Relentless; unyielding (10)
Shackle (6)
Shocking (9)
Spacious; roomy (9)
Steep (11)
Stolen (9)
Stubborn (8)
Suitable; practical (9)
Unchanging (9)
Urgings (12)
Whim (7)

Frankenstein Vocabulary Word Search 1 Answer Key

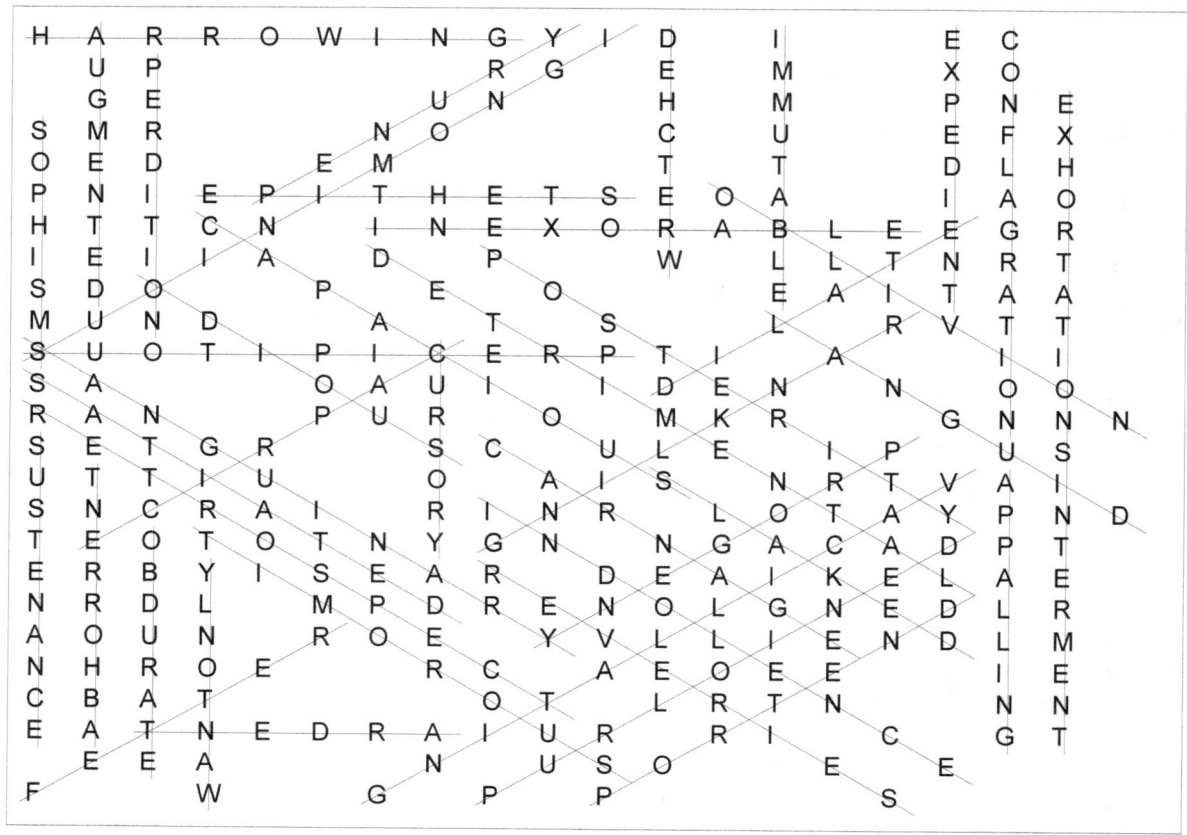

A great fire (13)
Abusive words (8)
Accompanied by carnage; bloodthirsty (10)
Burial (9)
Children; offspring (7)
Complete ruin (9)
Daydreams (8)
Destruction or wreckage of life (7)
Disgraceful (11)
Distressing; agonizing (9)
Expand (6)
Extreme poverty (6)
Fearful (8)
Fluctuating; wavering (11)
Forgotten; forgetfulness (8)
Fully satisfied (8)
Future generations (9)
Harmful; damaging (11)
Hastily done (7)
Hateful (6)
Hateful; detestable (9)
Immorally; cruelly (8)
Increased; added to (9)

Irritating (8)
Lacking energy (7)
Laziness (9)
Looking back on the past (10)
Means of nourishment (10)
Miserable (8)
Misleading arguments (8)
Passionate; enthusiastic (6)
Predict (7)
Quenched (6)
Relentless; unyielding (10)
Shackle (6)
Shocking (9)
Spacious; roomy (9)
Steep (11)
Stolen (9)
Stubborn (8)
Suitable; practical (9)
Unchanging (9)
Urgings (12)
Whim (7)

Frankenstein Vocabulary Word Search 2

```
O D P H Y S I O G N O M Y C C I M Q V R
B E O B L I T E R A T E D U O M T G P F
L T Y R A N I U G N A S M R U M C L H C
I R S M M M L N H R S F S N U E T C H
V I J O N V I W E D D X J O T T P E A Q
I M W V P W G T E E G L Y R E A S T P T
O E B T O H T N B I Z C E Y N B O A R N
N N T R D E I I V P N H X J A L R L I Y
C T R B F O L S S E E T P B N E T I C D
R A N K L I N G M L W R E T C H E D E W
H L P R T Q N E X S A N D R E S R G L C
W T U A Z S L D X B E K I I M B P Z B Z
W P T N C C U S O V D S E D T E S I A N
V E N O N I L S O L U H N D P I N H R W
D K E I P Y O L T O E E T H C D O T O W
I A D T T O E U R E T N W B E I I N X J
U P R A Q N S O S R N S C F A A T P E N
G P A R T B M T O D T A A E U B A A N T
N A C G E I P P E E W T N Y G O T R I B
A L R A T V F E H R I H N C M L R O O V
L L L L R K E T N G I E J J E I O X D Q
J I V F F N I R A U G T S D N C H Y I G
Q N W N B P A B I O R G Y D T A X S O P
Y G J O E P L G R E R Y S B E L E M U C
S J Y C L E L P E V S Y F L D L N X S M
```

A great fire (13)
Abusive words (8)
Accompanied by carnage; bloodthirsty (10)
Burial (9)
Children; offspring (7)
Complete ruin (9)
Daydreams (8)
Destroyed completely (11)
Destruction or wreckage of life (7)
Devilish (10)
Distressing; agonizing (9)
Expand (6)
Extreme poverty (6)
Face (11)
Facial features (11)
Fearful (8)
Forgotten; forgetfulness (8)
Future generations (9)
Generous (10)
Harmful; damaging (11)
Hastily done (7)
Hateful (6)
Increased; added to (9)

Irritating (8)
Lacking energy (7)
Laziness (9)
Looking back on the past (10)
Means of nourishment (10)
Miserable (8)
Misleading arguments (8)
Passionate; enthusiastic (6)
Predict (7)
Quenched (6)
Relentless; unyielding (10)
Shackle (6)
Shocking (9)
Spacious; roomy (9)
Spasm; convulsion (8)
Stolen (9)
Storminess (10)
Suitable; practical (9)
Tireless (13)
Unchanging (9)
Urgings (12)
Weakened; made unable (11)
Whim (7)

Frankenstein Vocabulary Word Search 2

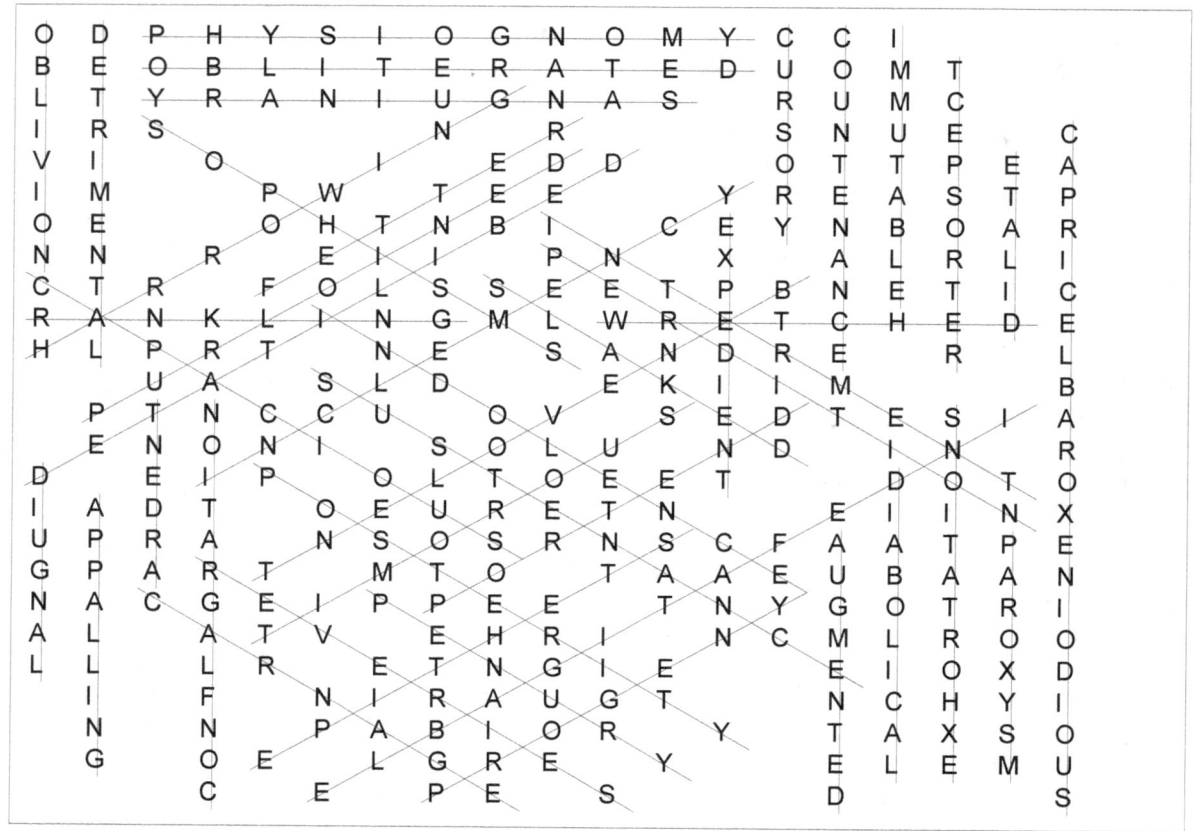

A great fire (13)
Abusive words (8)
Accompanied by carnage; bloodthirsty (10)
Burial (9)
Children; offspring (7)
Complete ruin (9)
Daydreams (8)
Destroyed completely (11)
Destruction or wreckage of life (7)
Devilish (10)
Distressing; agonizing (9)
Expand (6)
Extreme poverty (6)
Face (11)
Facial features (11)
Fearful (8)
Forgotten; forgetfulness (8)
Future generations (9)
Generous (10)
Harmful; damaging (11)
Hastily done (7)
Hateful (6)
Increased; added to (9)

Irritating (8)
Lacking energy (7)
Laziness (9)
Looking back on the past (10)
Means of nourishment (10)
Miserable (8)
Misleading arguments (8)
Passionate; enthusiastic (6)
Predict (7)
Quenched (6)
Relentless; unyielding (10)
Shackle (6)
Shocking (9)
Spacious; roomy (9)
Spasm; convulsion (8)
Stolen (9)
Storminess (10)
Suitable; practical (9)
Tireless (13)
Unchanging (9)
Urgings (12)
Weakened; made unable (11)
Whim (7)

Frankenstein Vocabulary Word Search 3

```
A P P A L L I N G C O D I O U S X X P K
B H X J O D B X S U O I N I M O N G I D
H R C V B D P L F R V A T P R Y F Y E W
O E D W D B V Q T S S B N C M T C T K J
R P Y A U T E I K O L O D F B I A I H Y
R U P N R B T N W R X L X P L R D M P C
E G E T A W J E E Y K I F X E E X A B M
N N R O T P G X R V Q C W T C T H L G L
T A D N E N U O R C O A I F D S B A S S
G N I L K N A R P O B L I V I O N C U J
N C T Y G K E A L C B F E N L P T O S B
I E I F B T R B C O F M D N A V I M T V
W B O Q T O J L B Z I O M B T R C M E Y
O Y N E X T R E D R L N Y J E A A I N P
R V F Y N N I E P E S R E P G U P S A H
R S S E V L K M N I U A M D A G R E N S
A M D L R A A C O N T I T T N M I R C T
H R S P L E E N E R D H N I R E C A E H
A P O S O T V P G E O E E P A N E T N D
P R P F J R Q E H U M U G T C T G E M H
Y O H B J M T C R R I M S Y S E E D D F
L G I D V Y T E E I Q D Z X V D X D T T
R E S B Q E W T N M E X P E D I E N T V
N N M D R T N F R D Q S U O I C A P A C
X Y S W S I S A N G U I N A R Y S Q T S
```

ABHORRENT	COMMISERATE	IMPERIOUS	PAROXYSM	REVERIES
APPALLING	CURSORY	INDOLENCE	PENURY	SANGUINARY
ARDENT	DIABOLICAL	INEXORABLE	PERDITION	SATIATED
AUGMENTED	DILATE	INTERMENT	PORTEND	SLAKED
BENEVOLENT	EPITHETS	LANGUID	POSTERITY	SOPHISMS
CALAMITY	EXPEDIENT	OBDURATE	PROGENY	SUSTENANCE
CAPACIOUS	FETTER	OBLITERATED	PURLOINED	TIMOROUS
CAPRICE	HARROWING	OBLIVION	RANKLING	WANTONLY
CARNAGE	IGNOMINIOUS	ODIOUS	REPUGNANCE	WRETCHED

Frankenstein Vocabulary Word Search 3 Answer Key

ABHORRENT	COMMISERATE	IMPERIOUS	PAROXYSM	REVERIES
APPALLING	CURSORY	INDOLENCE	PENURY	SANGUINARY
ARDENT	DIABOLICAL	INEXORABLE	PERDITION	SATIATED
AUGMENTED	DILATE	INTERMENT	PORTEND	SLAKED
BENEVOLENT	EPITHETS	LANGUID	POSTERITY	SOPHISMS
CALAMITY	EXPEDIENT	OBDURATE	PROGENY	SUSTENANCE
CAPACIOUS	FETTER	OBLITERATED	PURLOINED	TIMOROUS
CAPRICE	HARROWING	OBLIVION	RANKLING	WANTONLY
CARNAGE	IGNOMINIOUS	ODIOUS	REPUGNANCE	WRETCHED

Frankenstein Vocabulary Word Search 4

```
P I N E X O R A B L E T O B D U R A T E
O R R M Q P Y P L D N D I B G I N Q H H
R P E N U R Y D D E I S F M L W L R W J
T Y V C B P W V L O U C T E O I K A S P
E G E B I D O O U O B Z A S T R V U T Y
N T R P Y P V S I K X N U P S T O I Z E
D J I X I E I R T X Z O T T R I E U O S
Y J E M N G B T C E I C N F R I X R S N
S M S E G U N G O C R E C E P I C R K V
V S B P L Y N O A U M I P N E N D E P W
H Y L A P I P P M R S M T P Y C Q X T V
Z X S G L N A N E I I J I Y L L W H W R
Q O C K H C B T L B N T S M J E B O A Z
H R N Q K V N K P S H I P T X M Q R N Y
C A L A M I T Y R E T R O S P E C T T T
R P R P H F X S T C R G B U K N I A O S
Z I X R M C C S L N A D L S S C N T N S
P S M A O A D W R A P I I A M Y D I L G
S R B M R W X B S N P U T T S Y O O Y Q
D L O N U D I G B E A G E I I R L N H S
S J A G H T E N M T L N R A H O E S B P
Q G Y K E C A N G S L A A T P S N V F N
E W T Q E N F B T U I L T E O R C W F D
V T K T M D Y R L S N P E D S U E S H L
A U G M E N T E D E G J D E H C T E R W
```

APPALLING	EXHORTATIONS	OBDURATE	RANKLING
ARDENT	FETTER	OBLITERATED	RETROSPECT
AUGMENTED	HARROWING	OBLIVION	REVERIES
BENEVOLENT	IGNOMINIOUS	ODIOUS	SALUBRIOUS
CALAMITY	IMMUTABLE	PAROXYSM	SATIATED
CAPACIOUS	IMPERIOUS	PENURY	SLAKED
CAPRICE	INCLEMENCY	PERDITION	SOPHISMS
CARNAGE	INDOLENCE	PORTEND	SUSTENANCE
CURSORY	INEXORABLE	POSTERITY	TIMOROUS
DILATE	INTERMENT	PRECIPITOUS	WANTONLY
EPITHETS	LANGUID	PROGENY	WRETCHED

Frankenstein Vocabulary Word Search 4 Answer key

APPALLING	EXHORTATIONS	OBDURATE	RANKLING
ARDENT	FETTER	OBLITERATED	RETROSPECT
AUGMENTED	HARROWING	OBLIVION	REVERIES
BENEVOLENT	IGNOMINIOUS	ODIOUS	SALUBRIOUS
CALAMITY	IMMUTABLE	PAROXYSM	SATIATED
CAPACIOUS	IMPERIOUS	PENURY	SLAKED
CAPRICE	INCLEMENCY	PERDITION	SOPHISMS
CARNAGE	INDOLENCE	PORTEND	SUSTENANCE
CURSORY	INEXORABLE	POSTERITY	TIMOROUS
DILATE	INTERMENT	PRECIPITOUS	WANTONLY
EPITHETS	LANGUID	PROGENY	WRETCHED

Frankenstein Vocabulary Crossword 1

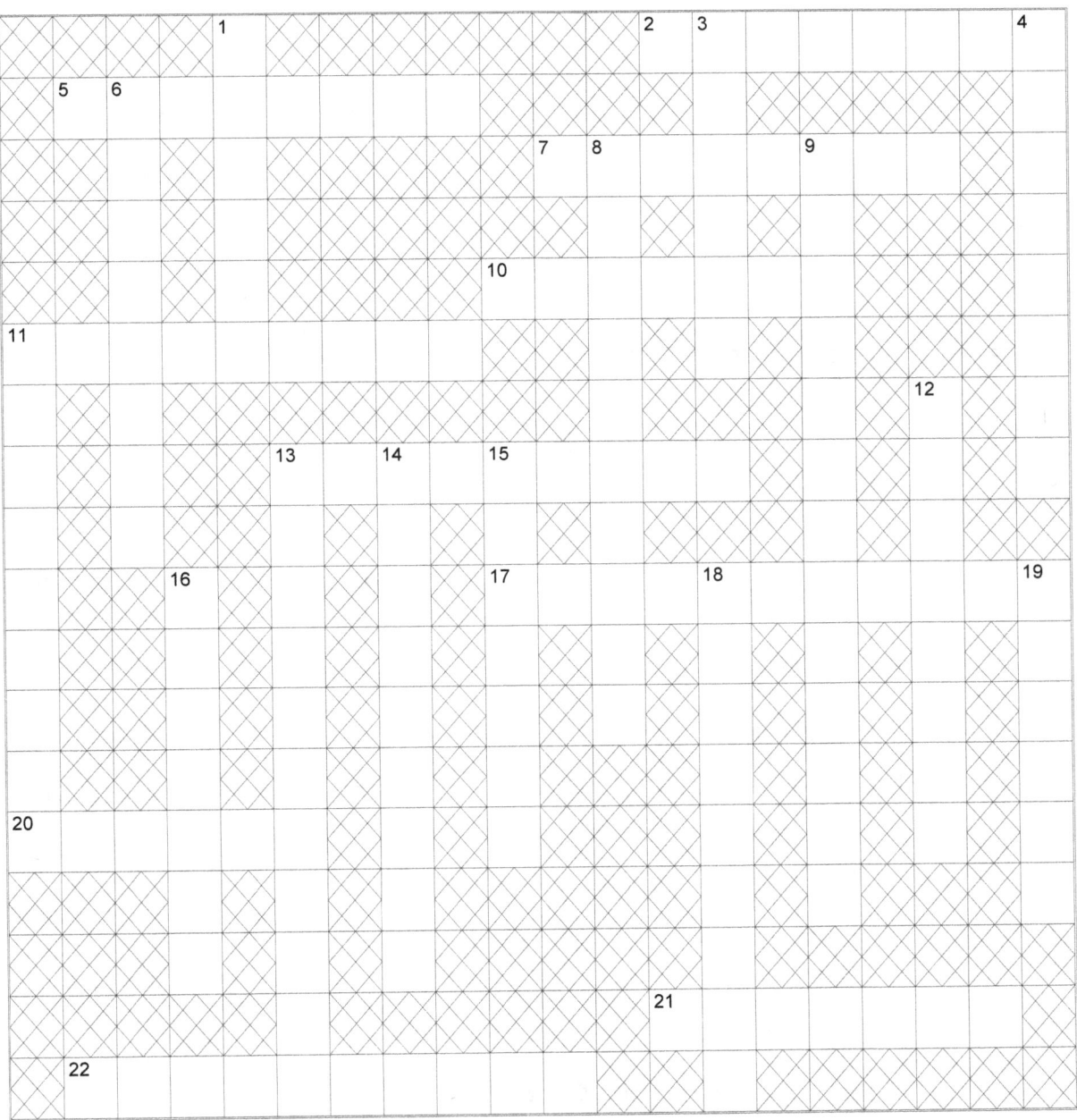

Across
2. Misleading arguments
5. Daydreams
7. Forgotten; forgetfulness
10. Lacking energy
11. Hateful; detestable
13. Spacious; roomy
17. Steep
20. Expand
21. Hastily done
22. Means of nourishment

Down
1. Shackle
3. Hateful
4. Fully satisfied
6. Abusive words
8. Generous
9. Tireless
11. Increased; added to
12. Spasm; convulsion
13. Feel sympathy for
14. Complete ruin
15. Whim
16. Destruction or wreckage of life
18. Domineering
19. Quenched

Frankenstein Vocabulary Crossword 1 Answer Key

Across
2. Misleading arguments
5. Daydreams
7. Forgotten; forgetfulness
10. Lacking energy
11. Hateful; detestable
13. Spacious; roomy
17. Steep
20. Expand
21. Hastily done
22. Means of nourishment

Down
1. Shackle
3. Hateful
4. Fully satisfied
6. Abusive words
8. Generous
9. Tireless
11. Increased; added to
12. Spasm; convulsion
13. Feel sympathy for
14. Complete ruin
15. Whim
16. Destruction or wreckage of life
18. Domineering
19. Quenched

Frankenstein Vocabulary Crossword 2

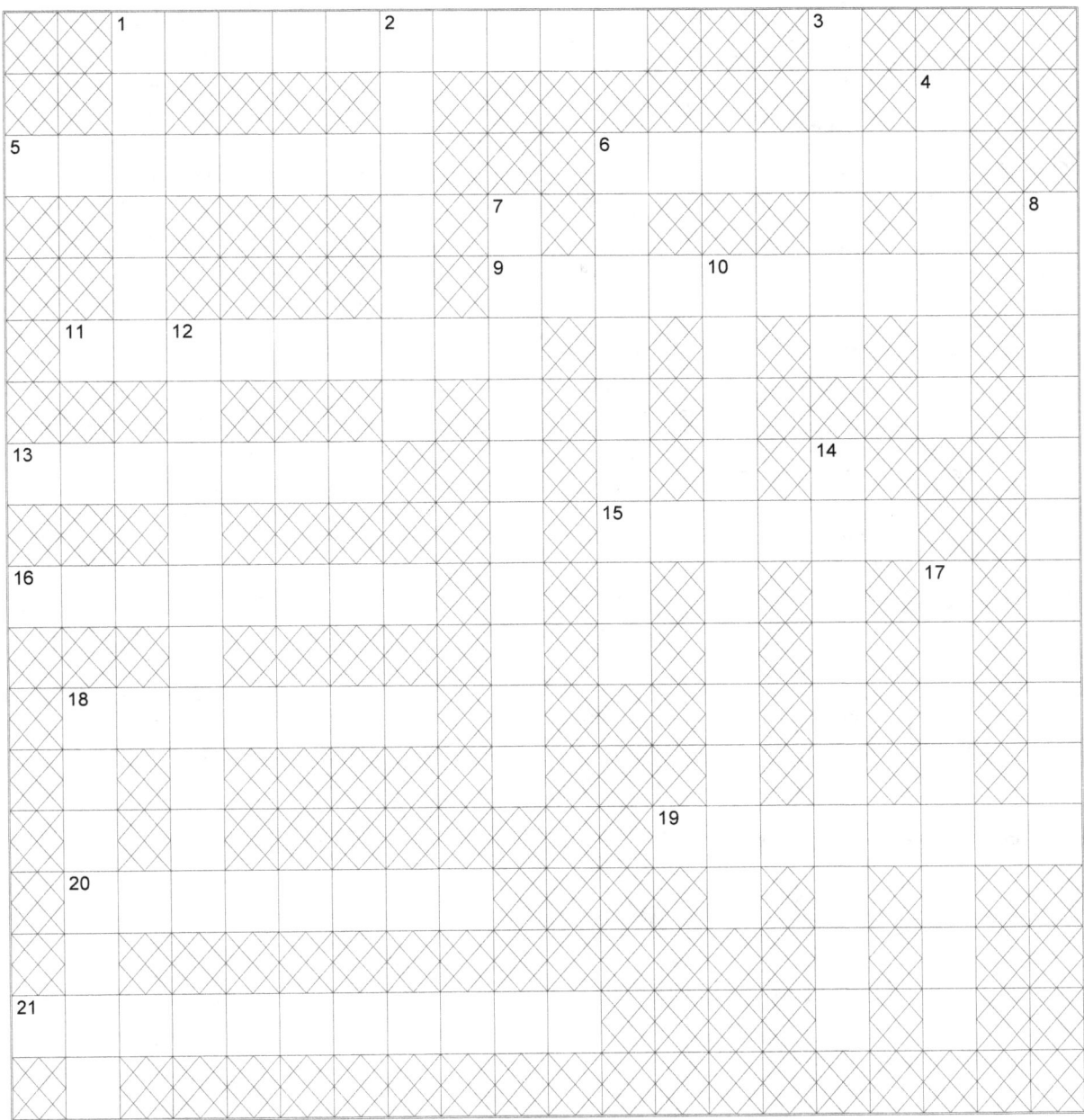

Across
1. Devilish
5. Forgotten; forgetfulness
6. Destruction or wreckage of life
9. Suitable; practical
11. Complete ruin
13. Predict
15. Hateful
16. Spasm; convulsion
18. Whim
19. Disaster
20. Fully satisfied
21. Steep

Down
1. Expand
2. Lacking energy
3. Quenched
4. Shackle
6. Spacious; roomy
7. Generous
8. Face
10. Harmful; damaging
12. Looking back on the past
14. Means of nourishment
17. Misleading arguments
18. Hastily done

Frankenstein Vocabulary Crossord 2 Answer Key

		¹D	I	A	B	O	²L	I	C	A	L			³S			
		I					A							L		⁴F	
⁵O	B	L	I	V	I	O	N		⁶C	A	R	N	A	G	E		
		A					G		⁷B	A				K		T	⁸P
		T					U		⁹E	X	P	¹⁰E	D	I	E	N	T	H
	¹¹P	¹²E	R	D	I	T	I	O	N			A				E		Y
		E				D		E			C		T			R		S
¹³P	O	R	T	E	N	D		V			I		R		¹⁴S			I
		R						O		¹⁵O	D	I	O	U	S			O
¹⁶P	A	R	O	X	Y	S	M		L		U		M		S		¹⁷S		G
		S							E		S		E		T		O		N
	¹⁸C	A	P	R	I	C	E		N				N		E		P		O
	U		E						T				T		N		H		M
	R		C								¹⁹C	A	L	A	M	I	T	Y
	²⁰S	A	T	I	A	T	E	D			L		N				S		
	O										C						M		
²¹P	R	E	C	I	P	I	T	O	U	S			E				S		
	Y																		

Across
1. Devilish
5. Forgotten; forgetfulness
6. Destruction or wreckage of life
9. Suitable; practical
11. Complete ruin
13. Predict
15. Hateful
16. Spasm; convulsion
18. Whim
19. Disaster
20. Fully satisfied
21. Steep

Down
1. Expand
2. Lacking energy
3. Quenched
4. Shackle
6. Spacious; roomy
7. Generous
8. Face
10. Harmful; damaging
12. Looking back on the past
14. Means of nourishment
17. Misleading arguments
18. Hastily done

Frankenstein Vocabulary Crossword 3

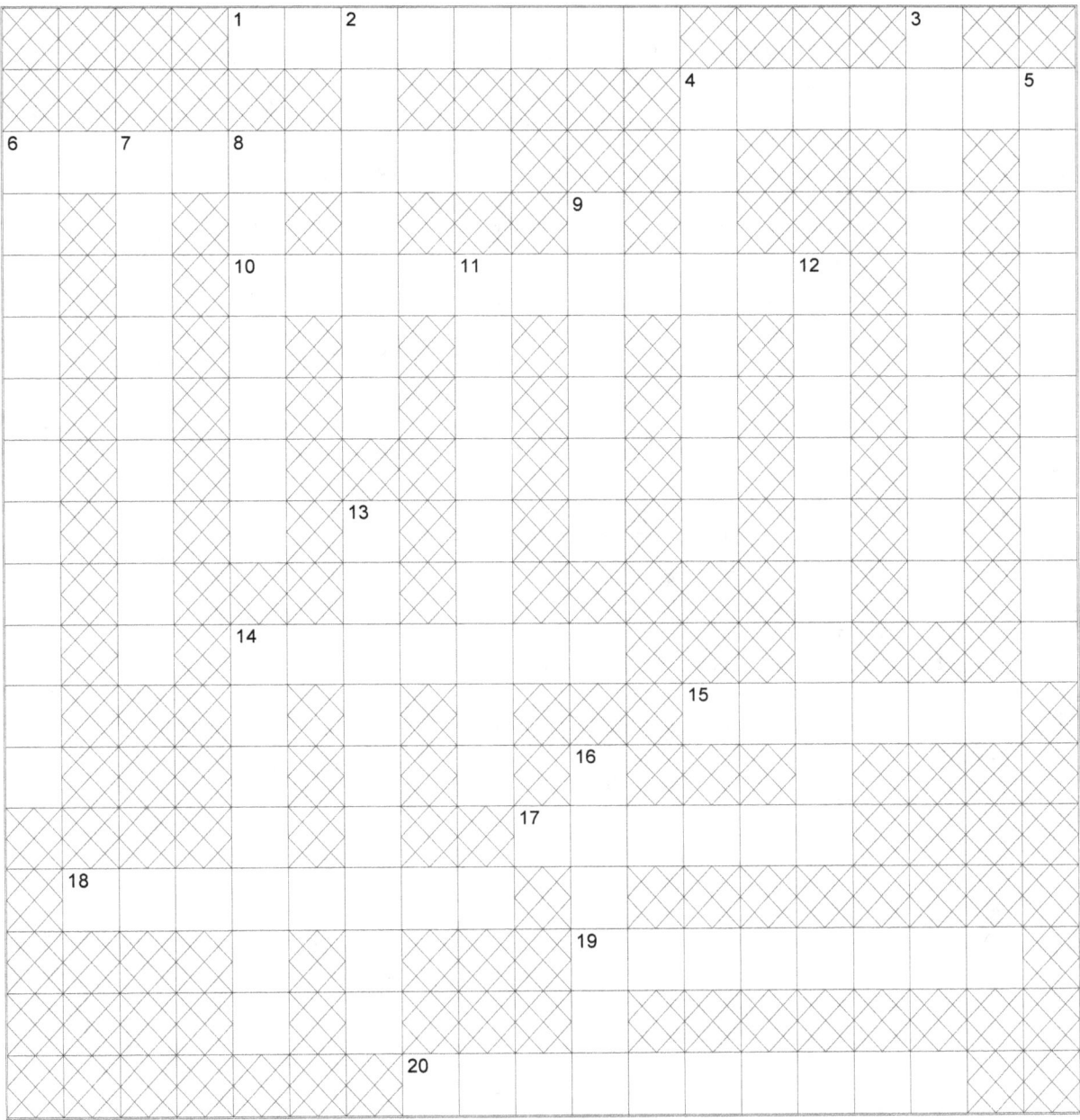

Across
1. Misleading arguments
4. Predict
6. Spacious; roomy
10. Steep
14. Hastily done
15. Quenched
17. Extreme poverty
18. Disaster
19. Fearful
20. Looking back on the past

Down
2. Children; offspring
3. Generous
4. Spasm; convulsion
5. Devilish
6. Feel sympathy for
7. Complete ruin
8. Whim
9. Expand
11. Domineering
12. Accompanied by carnage; bloodthirsty
13. Distressing; agonizing
14. Destruction or wreckage of life
16. Shackle

Frankenstein Vocabulary Crossword 3 Answer Key

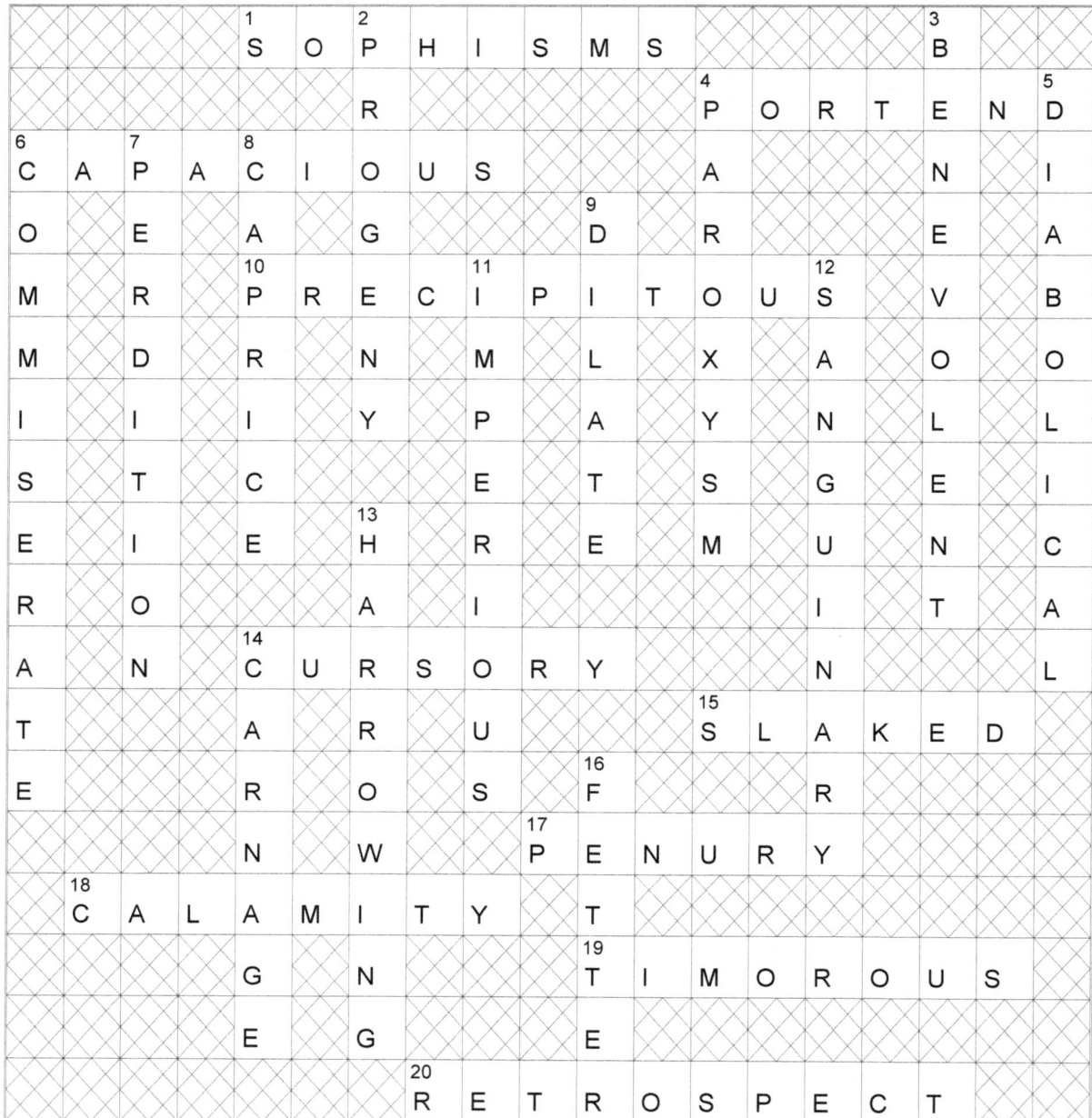

Across
1. Misleading arguments
4. Predict
6. Spacious; roomy
10. Steep
14. Hastily done
15. Quenched
17. Extreme poverty
18. Disaster
19. Fearful
20. Looking back on the past

Down
2. Children; offspring
3. Generous
4. Spasm; convulsion
5. Devilish
6. Feel sympathy for
7. Complete ruin
8. Whim
9. Expand
11. Domineering
12. Accompanied by carnage; bloodthirsty
13. Distressing; agonizing
14. Destruction or wreckage of life
16. Shackle

Frankenstein Vocabulary Crossword 4

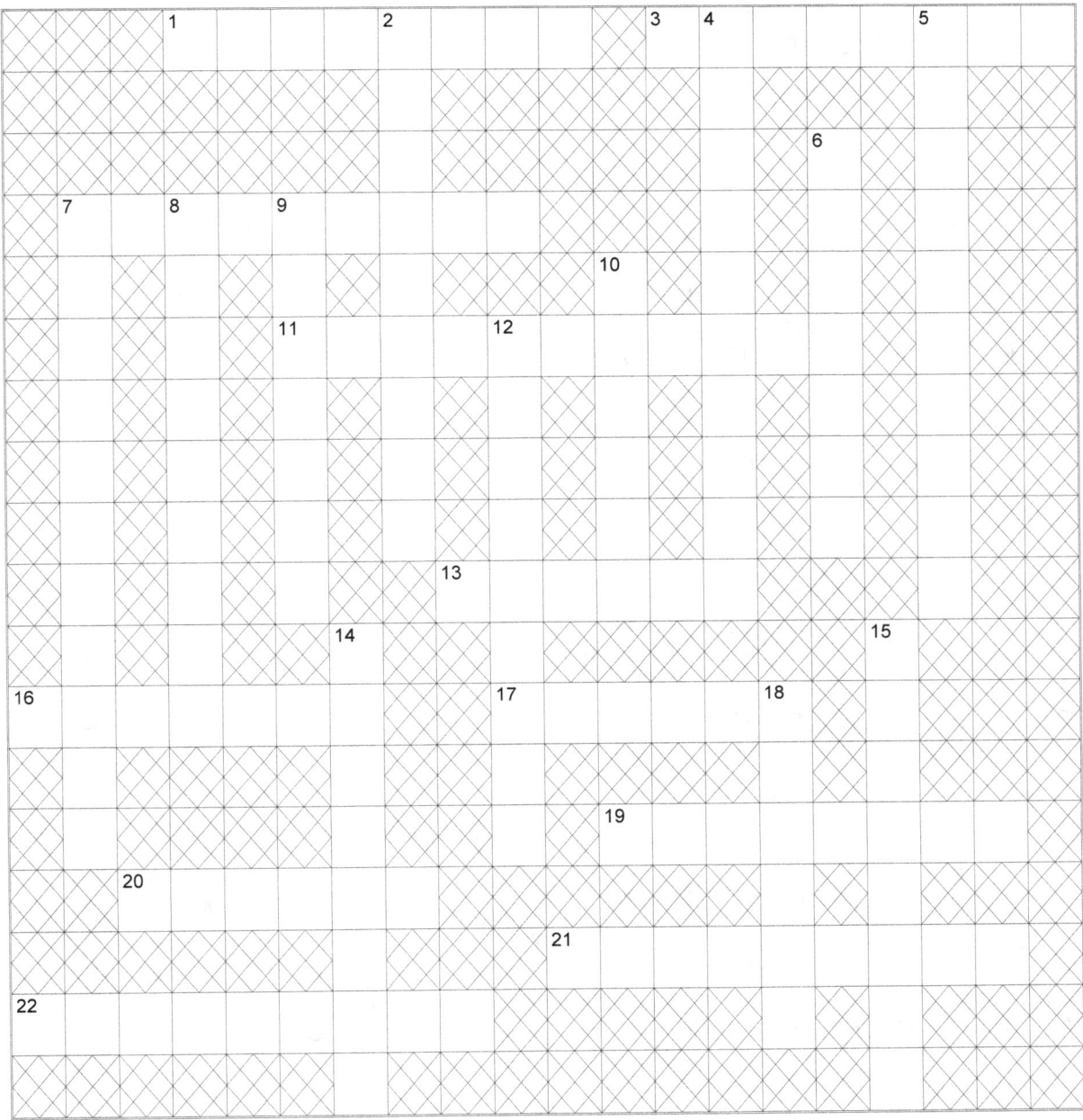

Across
1. Misleading arguments
3. Forgotten; forgetfulness
7. Spacious; roomy
11. Steep
13. Passionate; enthusiastic
16. Destruction or wreckage of life
17. Hateful
19. Disaster
20. Extreme poverty
21. Increased; added to
22. Hateful; detestable

Down
2. Laziness
4. Generous
5. Storminess
6. Hastily done
7. Feel sympathy for
8. Complete ruin
9. Whim
10. Expand
12. Domineering
14. Daydreams
15. Fully satisfied
18. Quenched

Frankenstein Vocabulary Crossword 4 Answer Key

Across
1. Misleading arguments
3. Forgotten; forgetfulness
7. Spacious; roomy
11. Steep
13. Passionate; enthusiastic
16. Destruction or wreckage of life
17. Hateful
19. Disaster
20. Extreme poverty
21. Increased; added to
22. Hateful; detestable

Down
2. Laziness
4. Generous
5. Storminess
6. Hastily done
7. Feel sympathy for
8. Complete ruin
9. Whim
10. Expand
12. Domineering
14. Daydreams
15. Fully satisfied
18. Quenched

Frankenstein Vocabulary Juggle Letters 1

1. OYSRCUR = 1. _____
   Hastily done

2. UPAAIOCSC = 2. _____
   Spacious; roomy

3. EOLINDNCE = 3. _____
   Laziness

4. PSHSMOSI = 4. _____
   Misleading arguments

5. DRNOTPIEI = 5. _____
   Complete ruin

6. CHDETWER = 6. _____
   Miserable

7. EURPYN = 7. _____
   Extreme poverty

8. AOLILCABDI = 8. _____
   Devilish

9. TTEIIBEADLD = 9. _____
   Weakened; made unable

10. COPRTSEERT =10. _____
    Looking back on the past

11. TEUANCNECON =11. _____
    Facial features

12. ESRRVEEI =12. _____
    Daydreams

13. OILIVONB =13. _____
    Forgotten; forgetfulness

14. OXSMAYRP =14. _____
    Spasm; convulsion

15. OYTIETSPR =15. _____
    Future generations

Frankenstein Vocabulary Juggle Letters 1 Answer Key

1. OYSRCUR = 1. CURSORY
   Hastily done

2. UPAAIOCSC = 2. CAPACIOUS
   Spacious; roomy

3. EOLINDNCE = 3. INDOLENCE
   Laziness

4. PSHSMOSI = 4. SOPHISMS
   Misleading arguments

5. DRNOTPIEI = 5. PERDITION
   Complete ruin

6. CHDETWER = 6. WRETCHED
   Miserable

7. EURPYN = 7. PENURY
   Extreme poverty

8. AOLILCABDI = 8. DIABOLICAL
   Devilish

9. TTEIIBEADLD = 9. DEBILITATED
   Weakened; made unable

10. COPRTSEERT =10. RETROSPECT
    Looking back on the past

11. TEUANCNECON =11. COUNTENANCE
    Facial features

12. ESRRVEEI =12. REVERIES
    Daydreams

13. OILIVONB =13. OBLIVION
    Forgotten; forgetfulness

14. OXSMAYRP =14. PAROXYSM
    Spasm; convulsion

15. OYTIETSPR =15. POSTERITY
    Future generations

Frankenstein Vocabulary Juggle Letters 2

1. EUAITMMBL = 1. _____
   Unchanging

2. LEBNTVENEO = 2. _____
   Generous

3. SOXRYMPA = 3. _____
   Spasm; convulsion

4. ETNTMERNI = 4. _____
   Burial

5. RWHECTDE = 5. _____
   Miserable

6. EPXETIDNE = 6. _____
   Suitable; practical

7. DNEART = 7. _____
   Passionate; enthusiastic

8. ITESOCRIPPU = 8. _____
   Steep

9. EIERSVRE = 9. _____
   Daydreams

10. APUECRGNEN = 10. _____
    Loathing; repulsiveness

11. ELIMENTTRAD = 11. _____
    Harmful; damaging

12. MNCIYNLECE = 12. _____
    Storminess

13. NYTWLOAN = 13. _____
    Immorally; cruelly

14. PCIUCAOSA = 14. _____
    Spacious; roomy

15. UBTDROAE = 15. _____
    Stubborn

Frankenstein Vocabulary Juggle Letters 2 Answer Key

1. EUAITMMBL = 1. IMMUTABLE
Unchanging

2. LEBNTVENEO = 2. BENEVOLENT
Generous

3. SOXRYMPA = 3. PAROXYSM
Spasm; convulsion

4. ETNTMERNI = 4. INTERMENT
Burial

5. RWHECTDE = 5. WRETCHED
Miserable

6. EPXETIDNE = 6. EXPEDIENT
Suitable; practical

7. DNEART = 7. ARDENT
Passionate; enthusiastic

8. ITESOCRIPPU = 8. PRECIPITOUS
Steep

9. EIERSVRE = 9. REVERIES
Daydreams

10. APUECRGNEN = 10. REPUGNANCE
Loathing; repulsiveness

11. ELIMENTTRAD = 11. DETRIMENTAL
Harmful; damaging

12. MNCIYNLECE = 12. INCLEMENCY
Storminess

13. NYTWLOAN = 13. WANTONLY
Immorally; cruelly

14. PCIUCAOSA = 14. CAPACIOUS
Spacious; roomy

15. UBTDROAE = 15. OBDURATE
Stubborn

Frankenstein Vocabulary Juggle Letters 3

1. ERTSPRTECO = 1. _____
   Looking back on the past

2. AURSLIUOSB = 2. _____
   Healthful

3. BLAEUTMIM = 3. _____
   Unchanging

4. LTNANYOW = 4. _____
   Immorally; cruelly

5. TDDEIIABETL = 5. _____
   Weakened; made unable

6. AEKSDL = 6. _____
   Quenched

7. NDETRA = 7. _____
   Passionate; enthusiastic

8. IRNNSUAAYG = 8. _____
   Accompanied by carnage; bloodthirsty

9. TRONARHBE = 9. _____
   Hateful; detestable

10. PRISOTEYT =10. _____
    Future generations

11. MEOPRIIUS =11. _____
    Domineering

12. EILEGDIBFNATA =12. _____
    Tireless

13. LARNGINK =13. _____
    Irritating

14. EESRREIV =14. _____
    Daydreams

15. OMOTRSIU =15. _____
    Fearful

Frankenstein Vocabulary Juggle Letters 3 Answer Key

1. ERTSPRTECO = 1. RETROSPECT
Looking back on the past

2. AURSLIUOSB = 2. SALUBRIOUS
Healthful

3. BLAEUTMIM = 3. IMMUTABLE
Unchanging

4. LTNANYOW = 4. WANTONLY
Immorally; cruelly

5. TDDEIIABETL = 5. DEBILITATED
Weakened; made unable

6. AEKSDL = 6. SLAKED
Quenched

7. NDETRA = 7. ARDENT
Passionate; enthusiastic

8. IRNNSUAAYG = 8. SANGUINARY
Accompanied by carnage; bloodthirsty

9. TRONARHBE = 9. ABHORRENT
Hateful; detestable

10. PRISOTEYT =10. POSTERITY
Future generations

11. MEOPRIIUS =11. IMPERIOUS
Domineering

12. EILEGDIBFNATA =12. INDEFATIGABLE
Tireless

13. LARNGINK =13. RANKLING
Irritating

14. EESRREIV =14. REVERIES
Daydreams

15. OMOTRSIU =15. TIMOROUS
Fearful

Frankenstein Vocabulary Juggle Letters 4

1. HISTTEPE = 1. _____
   Abusive words

2. UOSCPAACI = 2. _____
   Spacious; roomy

3. OTNIARLAGFOCN = 3. _____
   A great fire

4. RALOTTEDIBE = 4. _____
   Destroyed completely

5. EBEINFTIGDAAL = 5. _____
   Tireless

6. UIDNAGL = 6. _____
   Lacking energy

7. NDLPRIEUO = 7. _____
   Stolen

8. MITREENTADL = 8. _____
   Harmful; damaging

9. UDOIOS = 9. _____
   Hateful

10. DDAIIEETBLT =10. _____
    Weakened; made unable

11. DIRIETOPN =11. _____
    Complete ruin

12. AMBLIUEMT =12. _____
    Unchanging

13. RSPEITTOY =13. _____
    Future generations

14. AICTLMAY =14. _____
    Disaster

15. NAAGECR =15. _____
    Destruction or wreckage of life

Frankenstein Vocabulary Juggle Letters 4 Answer Key

1. HISTTEPE = 1. EPITHETS
   Abusive words

2. UOSCPAACI = 2. CAPACIOUS
   Spacious; roomy

3. OTNIARLAGFOCN = 3. CONFLAGRATION
   A great fire

4. RALOTTEDIBE = 4. OBLITERATED
   Destroyed completely

5. EBEINFTIGDAAL = 5. INDEFATIGABLE
   Tireless

6. UIDNAGL = 6. LANGUID
   Lacking energy

7. NDLPRIEUO = 7. PURLOINED
   Stolen

8. MITREENTADL = 8. DETRIMENTAL
   Harmful; damaging

9. UDOIOS = 9. ODIOUS
   Hateful

10. DDAIIEETBLT = 10. DEBILITATED
    Weakened; made unable

11. DIRIETOPN = 11. PERDITION
    Complete ruin

12. AMBLIUEMT = 12. IMMUTABLE
    Unchanging

13. RSPEITTOY = 13. POSTERITY
    Future generations

14. AICTLMAY = 14. CALAMITY
    Disaster

15. NAAGECR = 15. CARNAGE
    Destruction or wreckage of life

ABHORRENT	Hateful; detestable
APPALLING	Shocking
ARDENT	Passionate; enthusiastic
AUGMENTED	Increased; added to
BENEVOLENT	Generous
CALAMITY	Disaster

CAPACIOUS	Spacious; roomy
CAPRICE	Whim
CARNAGE	Destruction or wreckage of life
COMMISERATE	Feel sympathy for
CONFLAGRATION	A great fire
COUNTENANCE	Facial features

CURSORY	Hastily done
DEBILITATED	Weakened; made unable
DETRIMENTAL	Harmful; damaging
DIABOLICAL	Devilish
DILATE	Expand
EMACIATED	Thin and wasted

EPITHETS	Abusive words
EXHORTATIONS	Urgings
EXPEDIENT	Suitable; practical
FETTER	Shackle
HARROWING	Distressing; agonizing
IGNOMINIOUS	Disgraceful

IMMUTABLE	Unchanging
IMPERIOUS	Domineering
INCLEMENCY	Storminess
INDEFATIGABLE	Tireless
INDOLENCE	Laziness
INEXORABLE	Relentless; unyielding

INTERMENT	Burial
LANGUID	Lacking energy
OBDURATE	Stubborn
OBLITERATED	Destroyed completely
OBLIVION	Forgotten; forgetfulness
ODIOUS	Hateful

PAROXYSM	Spasm; convulsion
PENURY	Extreme poverty
PERDITION	Complete ruin
PHYSIOGNOMY	Face
PORTEND	Predict
POSTERITY	Future generations

PRECIPITOUS	Steep
PROGENY	Children; offspring
PROGNOSTICATED	Predicted
PURLOINED	Stolen
RANKLING	Irritating
REPUGNANCE	Loathing; repulsiveness

RETROSPECT	Looking back on the past
REVERIES	Daydreams
SALUBRIOUS	Healthful
SANGUINARY	Accompanied by carnage; bloodthirsty
SATIATED	Fully satisfied
SLAKED	Quenched

SOPHISMS	Misleading arguments
SUSTENANCE	Means of nourishment
TIMOROUS	Fearful
VACILLATING	Fluctuating; wavering
WANTONLY	Immorally; cruelly
WRETCHED	Miserable

Frankenstein Vocabulary

CALAMITY	OBLIVION	LANGUID	TIMOROUS	SUSTENANCE
SANGUINARY	CONFLAGRATION	PAROXYSM	CAPACIOUS	EXPEDIENT
COUNTENANCE	SALUBRIOUS	FREE SPACE	ODIOUS	DILATE
RANKLING	IMMUTABLE	PERDITION	APPALLING	DEBILITATED
OBLITERATED	CURSORY	ABHORRENT	CAPRICE	VACILLATING

Frankenstein Vocabulary

INDEFATIGABLE	WANTONLY	PROGNOSTICATED	SATIATED	REVERIES
BENEVOLENT	INDOLENCE	PHYSIOGNOMY	DIABOLICAL	INCLEMENCY
EPITHETS	RETROSPECT	FREE SPACE	FETTER	OBDURATE
POSTERITY	PENURY	REPUGNANCE	EXHORTATIONS	ARDENT
CARNAGE	PORTEND	PURLOINED	INEXORABLE	PROGENY

Frankenstein Vocabulary

PRECIPITOUS	SANGUINARY	OBDURATE	DIABOLICAL	WANTONLY
EMACIATED	OBLITERATED	VACILLATING	SLAKED	COMMISERATE
REVERIES	PURLOINED	FREE SPACE	SALUBRIOUS	DEBILITATED
SOPHISMS	INDEFATIGABLE	PHYSIOGNOMY	TIMOROUS	FETTER
AUGMENTED	CURSORY	PROGENY	CONFLAGRATION	INEXORABLE

Frankenstein Vocabulary

SUSTENANCE	ARDENT	LANGUID	SATIATED	IMPERIOUS
DETRIMENTAL	RETROSPECT	APPALLING	PERDITION	CALAMITY
ABHORRENT	IGNOMINIOUS	FREE SPACE	EXPEDIENT	OBLIVION
REPUGNANCE	COUNTENANCE	POSTERITY	INCLEMENCY	DILATE
RANKLING	INDOLENCE	CAPRICE	INTERMENT	PENURY

Frankenstein Vocabulary

ARDENT	INTERMENT	BENEVOLENT	PORTEND	RETROSPECT
FETTER	APPALLING	WANTONLY	EMACIATED	COUNTENANCE
PROGENY	OBLIVION	FREE SPACE	SUSTENANCE	DIABOLICAL
OBLITERATED	AUGMENTED	DEBILITATED	PERDITION	IMPERIOUS
CALAMITY	EXHORTATIONS	INDOLENCE	INCLEMENCY	LANGUID

Frankenstein Vocabulary

TIMOROUS	PURLOINED	PRECIPITOUS	PENURY	ABHORRENT
EPITHETS	PAROXYSM	CONFLAGRATION	VACILLATING	DETRIMENTAL
CAPACIOUS	DILATE	FREE SPACE	SATIATED	SOPHISMS
CARNAGE	HARROWING	ODIOUS	IMMUTABLE	PHYSIOGNOMY
WRETCHED	EXPEDIENT	IGNOMINIOUS	REVERIES	RANKLING

Frankenstein Vocabulary

IMPERIOUS	APPALLING	WANTONLY	INEXORABLE	EXPEDIENT
PENURY	COMMISERATE	DETRIMENTAL	INDEFATIGABLE	BENEVOLENT
LANGUID	PRECIPITOUS	FREE SPACE	IMMUTABLE	REPUGNANCE
VACILLATING	DIABOLICAL	CURSORY	OBDURATE	CAPACIOUS
PERDITION	INCLEMENCY	ODIOUS	OBLITERATED	FETTER

Frankenstein Vocabulary

AUGMENTED	EPITHETS	PURLOINED	SATIATED	CAPRICE
ABHORRENT	PHYSIOGNOMY	REVERIES	OBLIVION	WRETCHED
PORTEND	ARDENT	FREE SPACE	POSTERITY	CARNAGE
INDOLENCE	TIMOROUS	EXHORTATIONS	SLAKED	IGNOMINIOUS
INTERMENT	PROGENY	HARROWING	SALUBRIOUS	CALAMITY

Frankenstein Vocabulary

SATIATED	IMMUTABLE	CALAMITY	FETTER	PHYSIOGNOMY
RANKLING	REVERIES	WRETCHED	HARROWING	CAPACIOUS
OBDURATE	DETRIMENTAL	FREE SPACE	DILATE	REPUGNANCE
SANGUINARY	PURLOINED	RETROSPECT	COUNTENANCE	CONFLAGRATION
PROGENY	AUGMENTED	DIABOLICAL	IGNOMINIOUS	LANGUID

Frankenstein Vocabulary

PAROXYSM	ARDENT	APPALLING	TIMOROUS	OBLITERATED
OBLIVION	EMACIATED	BENEVOLENT	COMMISERATE	INEXORABLE
PRECIPITOUS	INDOLENCE	FREE SPACE	CURSORY	CARNAGE
EXHORTATIONS	PENURY	VACILLATING	SALUBRIOUS	POSTERITY
INTERMENT	EPITHETS	PORTEND	EXPEDIENT	IMPERIOUS

Frankenstein Vocabulary

PHYSIOGNOMY	IGNOMINIOUS	CAPACIOUS	SANGUINARY	CONFLAGRATION
INEXORABLE	DIABOLICAL	HARROWING	ODIOUS	AUGMENTED
PAROXYSM	PERDITION	FREE SPACE	BENEVOLENT	ARDENT
OBDURATE	INDEFATIGABLE	COMMISERATE	TIMOROUS	EPITHETS
CARNAGE	ABHORRENT	APPALLING	CALAMITY	INDOLENCE

Frankenstein Vocabulary

PENURY	PROGENY	SATIATED	COUNTENANCE	REVERIES
FETTER	PROGNOSTICATED	PURLOINED	SLAKED	DETRIMENTAL
EXHORTATIONS	VACILLATING	FREE SPACE	RETROSPECT	WANTONLY
CURSORY	CAPRICE	EXPEDIENT	SOPHISMS	INTERMENT
REPUGNANCE	SUSTENANCE	DILATE	PRECIPITOUS	INCLEMENCY

Frankenstein Vocabulary

RETROSPECT	COUNTENANCE	REPUGNANCE	PROGENY	SATIATED
SALUBRIOUS	CAPRICE	OBLIVION	PURLOINED	EXPEDIENT
SUSTENANCE	AUGMENTED	FREE SPACE	SLAKED	INDOLENCE
EMACIATED	PHYSIOGNOMY	PROGNOSTICATED	PRECIPITOUS	DETRIMENTAL
ABHORRENT	IGNOMINIOUS	CARNAGE	CALAMITY	DILATE

Frankenstein Vocabulary

TIMOROUS	WANTONLY	WRETCHED	VACILLATING	APPALLING
SANGUINARY	FETTER	EPITHETS	DIABOLICAL	REVERIES
PORTEND	OBLITERATED	FREE SPACE	HARROWING	BENEVOLENT
COMMISERATE	IMPERIOUS	PENURY	CONFLAGRATION	ODIOUS
POSTERITY	INCLEMENCY	INEXORABLE	SOPHISMS	DEBILITATED

Frankenstein Vocabulary

SALUBRIOUS	IMMUTABLE	DETRIMENTAL	DIABOLICAL	OBLITERATED
SATIATED	ODIOUS	REPUGNANCE	TIMOROUS	CALAMITY
POSTERITY	PERDITION	FREE SPACE	CAPRICE	VACILLATING
SLAKED	PROGENY	PRECIPITOUS	LANGUID	INDEFATIGABLE
OBDURATE	RETROSPECT	IMPERIOUS	APPALLING	PROGNOSTICATED

Frankenstein Vocabulary

SANGUINARY	COMMISERATE	PAROXYSM	PENURY	SOPHISMS
COUNTENANCE	ARDENT	DILATE	REVERIES	INTERMENT
WRETCHED	EMACIATED	FREE SPACE	FETTER	INDOLENCE
SUSTENANCE	RANKLING	DEBILITATED	CAPACIOUS	HARROWING
CURSORY	EXPEDIENT	PHYSIOGNOMY	INEXORABLE	ABHORRENT

Frankenstein Vocabulary

IGNOMINIOUS	CURSORY	EPITHETS	INDEFATIGABLE	CARNAGE
AUGMENTED	SATIATED	PORTEND	OBDURATE	COUNTENANCE
PHYSIOGNOMY	WANTONLY	FREE SPACE	ODIOUS	COMMISERATE
REVERIES	POSTERITY	INTERMENT	PURLOINED	APPALLING
OBLITERATED	DETRIMENTAL	CONFLAGRATION	DEBILITATED	SLAKED

Frankenstein Vocabulary

CAPACIOUS	SUSTENANCE	EXPEDIENT	IMMUTABLE	HARROWING
TIMOROUS	IMPERIOUS	INDOLENCE	PAROXYSM	INEXORABLE
SALUBRIOUS	OBLIVION	FREE SPACE	DIABOLICAL	SOPHISMS
PENURY	REPUGNANCE	RETROSPECT	DILATE	CAPRICE
ARDENT	RANKLING	PROGENY	EXHORTATIONS	EMACIATED

Frankenstein Vocabulary

PERDITION	CURSORY	COUNTENANCE	APPALLING	PRECIPITOUS
PROGNOSTICATED	EMACIATED	SLAKED	COMMISERATE	SATIATED
TIMOROUS	PORTEND	FREE SPACE	EPITHETS	POSTERITY
EXPEDIENT	WRETCHED	LANGUID	VACILLATING	SANGUINARY
IMPERIOUS	CAPRICE	RANKLING	ODIOUS	ARDENT

Frankenstein Vocabulary

PHYSIOGNOMY	SOPHISMS	INTERMENT	PROGENY	REPUGNANCE
EXHORTATIONS	WANTONLY	PURLOINED	INEXORABLE	CALAMITY
INCLEMENCY	OBDURATE	FREE SPACE	DETRIMENTAL	DEBILITATED
PAROXYSM	SALUBRIOUS	OBLITERATED	CONFLAGRATION	DIABOLICAL
FETTER	CAPACIOUS	INDOLENCE	AUGMENTED	ABHORRENT

Frankenstein Vocabulary

SLAKED	IMPERIOUS	REVERIES	RETROSPECT	OBLITERATED
PAROXYSM	WANTONLY	PRECIPITOUS	COMMISERATE	CONFLAGRATION
LANGUID	OBDURATE	FREE SPACE	INTERMENT	PROGENY
AUGMENTED	PORTEND	WRETCHED	SATIATED	SANGUINARY
SOPHISMS	PROGNOSTICATED	DIABOLICAL	EMACIATED	HARROWING

Frankenstein Vocabulary

IGNOMINIOUS	CURSORY	POSTERITY	INCLEMENCY	ODIOUS
CALAMITY	OBLIVION	PURLOINED	CAPRICE	INDOLENCE
IMMUTABLE	INEXORABLE	FREE SPACE	EPITHETS	ARDENT
INDEFATIGABLE	EXPEDIENT	SUSTENANCE	ABHORRENT	SALUBRIOUS
CAPACIOUS	APPALLING	DEBILITATED	DETRIMENTAL	VACILLATING

Frankenstein Vocabulary

CARNAGE	RANKLING	EXHORTATIONS	ARDENT	EXPEDIENT
WANTONLY	WRETCHED	IGNOMINIOUS	APPALLING	PHYSIOGNOMY
INEXORABLE	SOPHISMS	FREE SPACE	IMMUTABLE	INCLEMENCY
VACILLATING	PENURY	EMACIATED	ODIOUS	INDOLENCE
CAPACIOUS	CAPRICE	DILATE	POSTERITY	PROGNOSTICATED

Frankenstein Vocabulary

PERDITION	HARROWING	PROGENY	ABHORRENT	CALAMITY
SLAKED	SATIATED	TIMOROUS	OBLIVION	PAROXYSM
CONFLAGRATION	FETTER	FREE SPACE	IMPERIOUS	OBDURATE
PRECIPITOUS	DETRIMENTAL	INDEFATIGABLE	INTERMENT	CURSORY
OBLITERATED	DIABOLICAL	SUSTENANCE	COUNTENANCE	COMMISERATE

Frankenstein Vocabulary

CAPRICE	EXHORTATIONS	SALUBRIOUS	AUGMENTED	INTERMENT
PERDITION	REPUGNANCE	WANTONLY	IGNOMINIOUS	EMACIATED
RETROSPECT	COMMISERATE	FREE SPACE	SATIATED	COUNTENANCE
CONFLAGRATION	VACILLATING	SANGUINARY	INCLEMENCY	PORTEND
HARROWING	OBLIVION	SLAKED	APPALLING	CURSORY

Frankenstein Vocabulary

ARDENT	SUSTENANCE	SOPHISMS	BENEVOLENT	DIABOLICAL
PROGENY	REVERIES	LANGUID	OBDURATE	TIMOROUS
EPITHETS	PENURY	FREE SPACE	RANKLING	PURLOINED
INDEFATIGABLE	EXPEDIENT	DEBILITATED	INEXORABLE	ABHORRENT
CARNAGE	PAROXYSM	DETRIMENTAL	PHYSIOGNOMY	FETTER

Frankenstein Vocabulary

INEXORABLE	EXPEDIENT	CURSORY	AUGMENTED	OBLITERATED
RETROSPECT	INDOLENCE	LANGUID	CARNAGE	TIMOROUS
INCLEMENCY	PROGNOSTICATED	FREE SPACE	PERDITION	ABHORRENT
SATIATED	IGNOMINIOUS	DEBILITATED	POSTERITY	BENEVOLENT
DIABOLICAL	EPITHETS	PROGENY	OBLIVION	COUNTENANCE

Frankenstein Vocabulary

ARDENT	COMMISERATE	SALUBRIOUS	HARROWING	RANKLING
OBDURATE	ODIOUS	PURLOINED	IMMUTABLE	SOPHISMS
PAROXYSM	IMPERIOUS	FREE SPACE	WANTONLY	CAPACIOUS
WRETCHED	INTERMENT	CALAMITY	FETTER	CAPRICE
EXHORTATIONS	PHYSIOGNOMY	EMACIATED	INDEFATIGABLE	SUSTENANCE

Frankenstein Vocabulary

INDEFATIGABLE	IGNOMINIOUS	BENEVOLENT	PRECIPITOUS	OBDURATE
LANGUID	DETRIMENTAL	CALAMITY	SALUBRIOUS	ARDENT
PAROXYSM	EXHORTATIONS	FREE SPACE	CURSORY	SUSTENANCE
OBLIVION	CAPACIOUS	TIMOROUS	COUNTENANCE	EXPEDIENT
PORTEND	ODIOUS	IMMUTABLE	INDOLENCE	OBLITERATED

Frankenstein Vocabulary

AUGMENTED	RANKLING	COMMISERATE	INEXORABLE	SANGUINARY
SLAKED	REVERIES	DILATE	PERDITION	VACILLATING
PROGNOSTICATED	WANTONLY	FREE SPACE	REPUGNANCE	IMPERIOUS
EMACIATED	PROGENY	CONFLAGRATION	SOPHISMS	FETTER
APPALLING	CAPRICE	POSTERITY	RETROSPECT	SATIATED

Frankenstein Vocabulary

INDEFATIGABLE	WANTONLY	EXHORTATIONS	AUGMENTED	OBLITERATED
OBLIVION	APPALLING	CAPACIOUS	DETRIMENTAL	IGNOMINIOUS
PHYSIOGNOMY	OBDURATE	FREE SPACE	SANGUINARY	SATIATED
CARNAGE	INTERMENT	EPITHETS	ABHORRENT	PURLOINED
CURSORY	SLAKED	CALAMITY	SOPHISMS	PROGNOSTICATED

Frankenstein Vocabulary

REVERIES	ARDENT	SALUBRIOUS	IMMUTABLE	TIMOROUS
RETROSPECT	HARROWING	IMPERIOUS	INDOLENCE	RANKLING
INEXORABLE	FETTER	FREE SPACE	WRETCHED	PROGENY
SUSTENANCE	BENEVOLENT	DEBILITATED	DIABOLICAL	COMMISERATE
PERDITION	INCLEMENCY	PENURY	PORTEND	COUNTENANCE

www.ingramcontent.com/pod-product-compliance
Lightning Source LLC
Chambersburg PA
CBHW081454070526
44586CB00019B/2350